MOTORBOOKS

WITHDRAWN

How to
Repair
Your Car

Paul Brand

Acknowlegments

A tip of the hat to Lee Klancher at Motorbooks for challenging me with the idea of writing this book. With MBI being located in St. Paul, Minnesota, Lee was familiar with my work as host of *AutoTalk* on AM 1500 KSTP and the "Motoring" columnist for the *Star Tribune* for the past 25 years.

Not having written a book before, I'll confess to being intimidated by the idea of having to sit down and write on a regular basis. Much to my pleasant surprise, most of the information was already on my mental "hard drive", and getting it down on paper—well, MS Word anyway—turned out not to be a chore.

Kris Palmer also gets a high-five for his input and creative captions, and my long-time friend Doug Dahlke, the sharpest professional car guy I've ever known, deserves a hearty thanks for reviewing the manuscript and troubleshooting guides and offering his input and expertise.

And finally, two-plus decades of heartfelt thanks to my wife, Jeri, for putting up with all the hours in the garage, all the grease stains on my pants, old parts in the laundry tub, bleeding brakes with me—starting on our honeymoon!—and keeping our race team watered and fed on the road all those years.

Automobiles can be intimidating in every respect, but trust me, they're not smarter than you are. If any of the information, troubleshooting guides, or tips helps save you a few bucks on your vehicle, good for you! And if you decide to actually work on your vehicle yourself, bust a knuckle—it's the badge of the motorhead!

A special thanks to the good people at the Dunwoody Institute, especially Automotive Department Director Chuck Bowen, for providing cars and a site to photograph the projects in the book, and to student workers Dan Moldan and Eric Anderson, who did the work shown in the photos. Dunwoody is one of the finest automotive technical teaching institutes in the country, and has been around almost as long as cars (they were founded in 1914!). Check them out at:

Dunwoody College of Technology
818 Dunwoody Boulevard
Minneapolis, MN 55403-1192
Phone (612) 374-5800 or 1-800-292-4625
Fax (612) 374-4128
Email info@dunwoody.edu
www.dunwoody.edu

Paul Brand *– Stanchfield, Minnesota*

First published in 2006 by Motorbooks, an imprint of MBI Publishing Company, Galtier Plaza, Suite 200, 380 Jackson Street, St. Paul, MN 55101-3885 USA

Copyright © 2006
by Paul Brand, Hector Cademartori, Jerry Lee, and Kris Palmer

The information in this book is true and complete to the best of our knowledge.

MBI Publishing Company titles are also available at discounts in bulk quantity for industrial or sales-promotional use. For details write to Special Sales Manager at MBI Publishing Company, Galtier Plaza, Suite 200, 380 Jackson Street, St. Paul, MN 55101-3885 USA

ISBN-13: 978-0-7603-2273-4
ISBN-10: 0-7603-2273-2

Editor: Lee Klancher
Designer: Rochelle Schultz Brancato

Printed in China

Library of Congress Cataloging-in-Publication Data

Brand, Paul, 1949-
    How to repair your car / Paul Brand.
    p. cm.
    ISBN-13: 978-0-7603-2273-4 (pbk. : alk. paper)
    ISBN-10: 0-7603-2273-2 (pbk. : alk. paper)
    1. Automobiles—Maintenance and repair—Amateurs' manuals. I. Title.
    TL152.B685 2006
    629.28'72--dc22
                            2006015530

Contents

Chapter 5   96
Cooling System

Chapter 6   128
Drivetrain

Chapter 7   152
Suspension and Steering

Chapter 8 · 165
Tires and Wheels

Chapter 9 · 180
Brakes

Chapter 10 · 202
Exhaust

Chapter 11 · 208
Caring for Your Car Interior and Exterior

CONTENTS

About the Authors

Paul Brand is well known and respected for his vast knowledge of automobiles. He's the host of *Autotalk*, a radio show devoted to automobiles, and an automotive columnist for the Minneapolis *Star Tribune*.

As an automotive troubleshooter, race-car driver, and leading instructor of law enforcement pursuit driving, Brand makes his shows and columns informative and entertaining with his wit, knowledge, and easy-to-understand advice on any and all auto problems. A typical show will find Brand expertly fielding questions about changing your own oil, finding the source of squeaks, squeals, and rattles or even deciphering the complex inner workings of an automatic transmission, an engine, or electronics.

One of Brand's goals is simply to help people understand more about automobiles so that they may get longer service life and be wiser customers. He is in great demand as a speaker at automotive conventions, trade shows, and anywhere there is a gathering of people connected with the automobile industry.

Brand resides in Lino Lakes, Minnesota.

Born in Buenos Aires, Argentina, **Hector Cademartori's** illustrations and paintings are sold to racing teams, corporations, magazines, and private parties. Cademartori's art can be found in Dan Gurney's All American Racers offices, Indianapolis 500 Yearbook covers, Laguna Seca Raceway, California Speedway, the Carrera Panamericana posters, NHRA offices, foreign and domestic automobile and motorcycle magazines, motorcycle manufacturers offices, and many other places. Hector Cademartori resides in La Verne, California with his wife, Florencia, and three children; Eduardo, Florencia, and Mercedes.

Automotive writer **Kris Palmer** writes for the *StarTribune* as well as MBI Publishing (*The Cars of the Fast and the Furious, Dream Garages*) when he's not restoring and hand fabricating parts for his Triumph TR6. Palmer brought his automotive knowledge and film directing talents to bear when working with photographer Jerry Lee to put together the 50 projects in the book.

Photographer **Jerry Lee** was the staff photographer for the University of Minnesota Sports Department for more then 10 years before going freelance in 2005. A lighting guru who has wired stadiums with flash systems, Lee's sense of light and composition were critical to making clear, easy-to-understand how-to photographs.

Introduction

Right now, are you in the back of the bookstore, hunched over this book, facing away from other customers so you won't be recognized? Are you a little self-conscious and don't want to be seen perusing a book on car repair and taking care of your automobile?

Never thought you'd be looking at a book like this, did you? For years, you just bought cars, put gas in them, drove them until you didn't want to anymore, then bought another one. At one time, new cars and trucks might have cost well under $10,000. In fact, the first new car I bought had a retail price of $2,675.

Today, the average family sedan costs 10 times that much! And with new car prices continuing to rise, it simply does not make economic sense to buy and drive a motor vehicle on a whim or because it has a flashy color.

Your car or truck may well be the single most expensive item you ever buy. Only the purchase of a home will top the number of dollars you'll spend on your automobile. And of course, your home will appreciate in value while your automobile will eventually end up in a salvage yard.

If you add up the costs of owning, operating, licensing, insuring, maintaining, and repairing your motor vehicle, the total will very likely top even the rent you're paying for your apartment or house.

If you are able and willing to buy a new car every three years or so, or to lease a new one, you may not need the help and information this book offers. But as you'll see in this book, there's a price—a very large price—for that convenience. If you would prefer to manage your money more tightly or are forced to because of budget constraints, it's more cost effective to keep your vehicle at least a year or two after the final payment. Or there's the other option: buy and drive pre-owned vehicles.

The way to save money on your car or truck is to be smart—car smart. Educate yourself, inform yourself, prepare yourself to efficiently and economically own and drive your automobile. Invest a little time and energy toward understanding what your vehicle needs from you in terms of care and maintenance, and how to diagnose and repair problems quickly and economically, whether you're a do-it-yourselfer or you have the work done by an automotive professional.

How much can you save? Would keeping several thousands of dollars in your pocket instead of spending it on your car be of interest to you?

A newer motor vehicle can easily cost $7,000–$10,000 per year to own and drive. Don't believe me? Add your monthly car payment, insurance premium, and fuel costs together, multiply by 12 for the yearly total, then add what you spent on maintenance, repairs, and service over the last 12 months.

Surprised? Don't be. Modern automobiles are expensive in every way. This book can help you control the cost of owning and driving your vehicle by helping you make good decisions on how to spend your automotive dollars.

Chapter 1
Basics and Troubleshooting

WARNING!

OLD SCHOOL TECH

TOMORROW'S TECH

KEY CONCEPT

MAINTENANCE TIP

MONEY-SAVING TIP

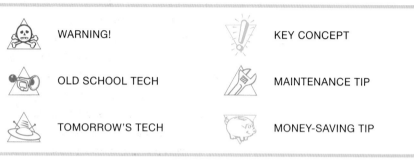

The basic idea behind this book is to demystify the modern automobile. As sophisticated as today's cars and trucks are, they still have four (or more) wheels and tires, an engine, a transmission, steering, brakes, and suspension systems. If you're willing to invest the time to read through the book, you'll learn how each system in your automobile works, and how to diagnose and troubleshoot problems with each system. No, you won't graduate as a master mechanic, but you will be able to walk the walk and talk the talk with automotive professionals. And you'll be able to maintain, service, and repair many of these systems yourself—if you choose to do so.

Each chapter deals with a major system in depth, and the troubleshooting guides help you identify and confirm specific problems or issues with that system. If your motor vehicle starts to behave differently, recognize that it could be the start of something big—as in expensive to repair. Use your eyes, ears, nose, and hands to identify what's happening, whether or not it's potentially serious, what might be the cause, how to confirm the diagnosis, and how to fix the problem—whether you fix it yourself or take it to a professional.

Hopefully this book will take the question marks out of vehicle ownership. By using this book as a dynamic reference, you'll know how to identify what might be wrong, what needs to be done to fix it, and how much it will cost.

Look at this book like you would a bank account. Invest your time and energy toward understanding your automobile, and your return on investment will be significant savings and better control of your automotive dollars.

And in today's world, that's a very good thing.

THE ICONS

This book uses six different icons to call attention to important parts of the text and to make it easier for you to find the information you need to get your car back on the road.

The icons are as follows:

Warning!
This is to alert you to dangerous chemicals or practices that you need to know while doing a procedure.

Old School Tech
Technical information that concerns older cars is flagged with this icon. If you are a bottom-line person, you can probably skip past this. If you are interested in history or have an older car, this information is for you.

Tomorrow's Tech

This signifies information on emerging technologies. This probably won't apply to your car today, but it might down the road.

Key Concept

These are the bottom-line explanations of how things work or how to fix things. If you want to quickly understand a system or process, turn to these.

Maintenance Tip

Tips on maintaining your car are marked with this icon. But you probably already got that, huh?

Money-Saving Tip

These tips are about moving your money from car maintenance to more worthy causes.

KNOW YOUR CAR

As a car owner, what's the most important asset you bring to vehicle ownership? Well, your wallet is right up there; motor vehicles are expensive to own, drive, and maintain. But without a doubt, the number one asset in controlling the cost of owning and driving your car or truck is to invest a little time and energy in knowing your vehicle—how to operate it, what it needs in terms of maintenance, and how to deal with issues or problems that arise.

For the most basic information—such as opening the fuel filler cap, locating the hood release handle or button, operating the defroster, setting the clock, even finding the space saver spare tire—the owner's manual supplied by the carmaker provides you with almost every piece of useful information you'll need to be a happy car owner.

In addition to all the fascinating operational tips to help you get the most from your vehicle, this little bible also covers all the maintenance requirements and intervals, identifies the owner-accessible components (such as fuses, jack, and jack handle), and explains all the warning lights and what you should do if they come on while driving.

There's an old saw that's popular with fleet managers. When the employee returns the company vehicle after several months or years of use, the manager asks whether he/she found the $10 bill hidden in the pages of the owner's manual. By gauging the reaction of the employee—a quick look back at the vehicle is a dead giveaway—the fleet manager knows whether the employee ever took the time to look through the owner's manual, thus whether or not the employee was focused on taking care of the company car.

No, you probably won't find a $10 bill in yours, but you will find all the information you need to successfully own and drive your vehicle, along with the information you'll need to take care of it for as long as you own it.

By the way, rumor has it that the vehicle is worth more when you sell or trade it if the owner's manual is still in the glove box. And you never know until you look—that $10 bill might still be there!

THE PREFLIGHT CHECK

Have you ever watched a professional pilot check out the aircraft he or she is about to fly? It's called a preflight check, and the idea is to have the pilot check the critical components on the aircraft—control surfaces and function, fuel tanks, landing gear, and the like—before climbing into the pilot's seat. Nice to know the wings are still attached properly before taking off, right? But perhaps more importantly, the preflight focuses the pilot's attention on the task at hand, safely operating the aircraft.

You may want to develop your own preflight for your vehicle.

No, of course you're not going to do this every time you drive the car, but it may be a good thing to do once a week on a vehicle you drive on a daily basis. It will keep you focused on taking care of your car and help you identify any problems at an early stage before they become serious or expensive.

A simple walk-around is a good habit to develop, where you visually confirm that the tires are in good condition and properly inflated, all the lights are intact and working, the wipers actually clear the windshield, and the exhaust, bodywork, and trim are in place and firmly attached. Pop the hood for a quick inspection of belts, hoses, radiator cap, and air cleaner, and check the key fluid levels like oil, transmission fluid, coolant, and brake fluid.

Here's my personal pet peeve: make sure all the glass is clean, inside and out. Fingerprints, greasy smears, dust, dirt, even doggy nose prints, will limit and distort, particularly at night, your view of the world around you, including traffic, cyclists, and pedestrians.

Speaking of safety, you don't need to be reminded of the importance of buckling your seatbelt, correct? Make sure you and every occupant of your vehicle are properly buckled up before you even start the engine.

And take a quick look around the cabin area. Secure or store any loose stuff. Remember, that 1-pound box of tissues sitting on the rear deck can become a 10-pound missile aimed at the back of your head in a 30-mile-per-hour frontal crash. The moral? Put the junk in the trunk.

WHAT YOU NEED IN A HOME SHOP

What's the absolutely best way to save money servicing your automobile? DIY, do it yourself! Shops and dealerships charge close to (if not more than!) $100 per hour for labor. Replace that with your free labor and you'll save a tremendous amount of money over the life of your vehicle.

No, you're not going to be able to overhaul that sophisticated automatic transmission in your garage, but you can take care of most of the basic maintenance and light repairs on your vehicle. This book has 50 projects that most people can do at home, showing you step-by-step ways to save time and money on your car. To do this work, you'll need a few basic tools and several pieces of useful equipment in your garage.

Here's the shopping list for what you'll need—it also makes a wonderful gift list.

- ☐ **Small, sturdy workbench with vice**
- ☐ **Floor jack and four jack stands**
- ☐ **Quality four-way lug wrench**
- ☐ **Bench-top/portable tool box**

- ☐ **Basic hand tools, including:**
  - ☐ 3/8-inch ratchet/socket set
  - ☐ 1/2-inch deep-well socket set, extension, breaker bar
  - ☐ SAE metric combination wrench set
  - ☐ Pliers—long nose, blunt nose, channel locks, and self-locking
  - ☐ Long flat blade
  - ☐ Digital tire pressure gauge
  - ☐ Tire tread depth indicator
  - ☐ Torque wrench—to properly tight wheel lugs
  - ☐ Plastic/paper oil/fluid funnel

- ☐ **Multi-bit screwdriver kit, including:**
  - ☐ Flat blade
  - ☐ Philips
  - ☐ Allen/hex

□ Torx/star
□ Square drive

If you want to impress all your friends and neighbors with your motor skills, add an air compressor to your wish list. You'll find that a compressor with basic air tools—impact wrench, air chuck, and blow nozzle—will be the most useful addition to your workshop.

Needless to say, it's easy to go overboard equipping your little garage shop, but the best plan is to start with the basics and add tools and equipment as necessary to service your specific vehicle.

HOW TO FIND A GOOD MECHANIC

Since you may not be equipped, inclined, or interested in a hands-on relationship with your automobile, it's critical that you identify a quality shop to help you care for your car. Whether it's the simple, routine maintenance like oil and filter changes, or diagnosing and troubleshooting a drivabilty issue with the engine, the key to successful and low-cost vehicle ownership is finding and keeping a good mechanic. In fact, as my wife discovered early on, marrying one is not a bad idea either!

If you're not inclined to look for that long-term relationship, at least find a shop and technician to service your vehicle. Obviously, if the vehicle is still covered under the carmaker or extended warranty, the dealership is the right place to go. No question, its technicians are qualified and experienced in servicing your particular make and model vehicle.

But what about simple maintenance items like oil changes? Is it necessary to go to the dealership? Or if the warranty is long gone, is the dealership the only place qualified to service your vehicle?

The answer to both questions is no. Obviously, the dealership is still a good choice for maintenance and repairs for the life of the car. And many car owners find the dealership a comfortable place to take their vehicle for service and repair. But service at the dealership often (not always, but often) costs more. And unless you live right around the corner, dealerships are usually a bit farther way than your local independent shop.

How do you find a good independent shop and technician to maintain and repair your vehicle? The same way you find the right car to buy in the first place: the test drive.

When it's time for your next oil change, stop by a shop in your area. Take advantage of any coupons or newspaper ads it may offer to attract you to the shop, and have it do a simple oil/filter/lube on your vehicle.

The $15–$25 you spend for the oil change will also buy you the opportunity to meet the owner or employees, check out the cleanliness and organization of the shop, check the certifications and credentials of the guys/gals working on your car, and find out if the shop fits your comfort zone.

Automotive Service Excellence (ASE) certification for the technicians is the national certification standard for automotive technicians. Look for the ASE certificate prominently displayed in the customer lounge.

If you're not entirely satisfied that this is *the* shop for you, try another shop at your next oil change or tire rotation or cooling system flush. Then another . . . and another . . . and another, until you find the right shop. It's just like shopping for any other major purchase; by test-driving a number of shops, you'll know the right one when you find it.

Also, don't forget to canvas your relatives, friends, coworkers, and acquaintances. Good recommendations from people you trust go a long, long way to helping establish your comfort zone for auto repair.

But remember: you have to ask. A satisfied customer has no reason to offer an opinion unless asked. A dissatisfied customer, on the other hand, protests and complains to anyone who will listen. At least you'll know which shops to avoid.

Once you find the right shop, hang onto to it and the folks who work there. Don't nitpick prices or service time. If it takes this shop an extra half-day to get the work done, or if it costs $25 more for a particular service, accept it with a smile on your face and don't forget to say "thank you." Remember these folks on holidays, and don't be afraid to tip them for exceptional service. Talk about seeing a surprised look on their faces! Even consider naming your first born after the shop.

Why? Because they'll step up to the plate with that extra effort when you need it. The next time your car's dead on the side of the road/stopped cold by a flat tire/won't start on a cold morning, if you've got a solid relationship with your favorite shop, they'll likely be willing to go the extra mile to help you.

Is it worth all this effort? You bet it is. Nothing, repeat nothing, will help you successfully and economically deal with the maintenance and service of your automobile better than a good relationship with a local full-service shop or dealership.

HOW TO TALK TO YOUR MECHANIC

By definition, a motorhead knows how to talk the talk and walk the walk. But for most car owners, the language used with modern automobiles might as well be Greek. If a technician told you your TPS was bad, locking out the O/D, and causing the MIL light to illuminate, would you understand what he or she was talking about? Would you know that replacing the TPS (throttle position sensor) should cost perhaps $200, not $700?

Knowing how to communicate with the technician or shop can be a huge asset in saving you money on car repair. Here's a classic example: Car owner brings car into shop complaining of dieseling. The technician warms car up, test drives it around the neighborhood, comes back to shop, shuts off the engine . . . and nothing. No popping, banging, sputtering, the engine stops cleanly. Customer picks up vehicle, but several days later comes back with the same complaint. Technician repeats process—still no dieseling when the engine is shut down.

Finally, the third time around and the customer thoroughly irritated, the tech climbs in the passenger seat and rides with the car owner for a test drive. Car owner drives out of the neighborhood to a winding road up a relatively steep grade. As car owner adds throttle to hold speed up the hill, the engine starts to rattle and ping from pre-ignition. "Hear that," says frustrated car owner, "it's dieseling."

The miscommunication between car owner and technician cost someone a considerably amount of time and money. If the shop didn't charge the car owner because it couldn't identify the problem, it costs the shop. If it did charge a diagnostic fee for its technician's time even though it didn't identify the problem, it costs the car owner.

By the way, the term "dieseling" is typically used to characterize the strange noises the engine makes when it does not actually stop running when the key is turned off. Residual heat and fuel can cause the engine to pop, bang, and sputter rather violently after shutdown. This doesn't happen as often with modern fuel injected engines, but it can be a startling, embarrassing situation for the unknowing car owner. Tip: The short-term solution is to leave the automatic transmission in gear to maintain a load on the engine, turn the key off, then shift into park, turn the ignition to lock, and remove the key.

Pre-ignition, or pinging, describes an uncontrolled explosion in the combustion chamber, rather than a smooth, progressive burning of the air/fuel mixture. The sound resembles a handful of small pebbles rattling around in a tin can. It's usually caused by inadequate octane fuel, but can also be attributed to overheating, carbon deposits, a lean air/fuel ratio, or ignition timing issues.

In this case, the difference between dieseling and pinging potentially costs the car owner lots of time and money in diagnostic costs, and the problem still is unresolved.

The moral of the story is: learn the lingo. Familiarize yourself with the terms and descriptions that best fit what you're vehicle is doing or not doing, as the case may be. The owner's manual is the place to start; you'll identify the correct names for the gizmos and whatchamacallits that you're concerned with. For example, you'll learn the difference between a fuse and a relay, you'll learn that PRNDL is the acronym for the transmission gearshift display—park, reverse, neutral, drive, and low.

Recognize that when your vehicle's behavior changes, something's happening. Most of the time, whatever is going on isn't particularly good and, if left unattended, usually gets worse. Don't ignore symptoms like squealing noises from the brakes, clicking or knocking noises from under the hood, strange smells, vibrations, or hesitations.

And rather than relying completely on verbal descriptions to the shop and/or your mechanic—which can leave the opportunity for misinterpretation—write down what you see, feel, smell, and/or hear and what circumstances or driving situations you experienced. Have the technician read through your notes with you, so that he or she is completely clear on what you're experiencing with your automobile.

Use the troubleshooting guides in this book to help orient yourself to the problem and its likely source. Vibrations can originate in the engine, belt-driven accessories, transmission, driveline, wheels, or tires. These troubleshooting guides will help you identify possible sources of the problem, narrow down the possibilities, and give you the information to provide to the shop so that it can pinpoint and fix the problem faster and at lower cost.

In fact, why not photocopy the specific troubleshooting guide, underline what you think the problem might be, and take it to the shop. Will the technicians be insulted, thinking you're trying to tell them how to do their job? Not in a good shop. They'll appreciate your efforts to focus on the problem and save them from wasting their time and your money.

If the issue is subtle—perhaps a light noise or vibration, but only at a certain speed or a certain grade or at a certain temperature—try to arrange to test drive the vehicle with the technician. If he or she experiences what you've experienced ("There, there it is. Feel that?"), you will have done a solid job of identifying the problem for the shop.

And guess what that will do? Save you money. The less time the tech spends figuring out what's wrong, the less the repair will cost. It's as simple as that.

COST OF OWNERSHIP

Depreciation is the single largest expense in owning and driving an automobile. Are you surprised? Unless you've purchased and driven a vehicle that's already 6–10 years old, the largest annual and overall cost to own and drive that car or truck is depreciation. Depreciation is the loss or reduction in value of the vehicle over the years and miles you drive it.

The best way to illustrate this cost is to compare the purchase price of the vehicle—whether new or used at the time of purchase—to the resale price of the vehicle at the time you sell or trade it. It's not at all uncommon for a vehicle priced at $25,000 new to be worth just $10,000 five years and 60,000 miles later. Do the simple math. That's $250 per month or $3,000 per year in depreciation. Compare this $57-plus cost per week to how much you spend on fuel, insurance, maintenance, and repair.

If you drive 15,000 miles per year and the vehicle averages 20 miles per gallon, you're going to burn roughly 750 gallons of fuel. At $2.50 per gallon, that's $1,875 per year, or $156.25 per month.

Maintenance and repairs? A budgeted $100 per month would give you a $1,200-per-year fund to take care of the vehicle. That should cover all but a catastrophic failure. Even bumping that to $150 per month would still put maintenance and repair well below depreciation in overall cost.

And how about insurance? Even on a new or newer vehicle with full coverage, monthly premiums are typically under $200 per month, $2,400 per year—unless, of course, your driving or claims record is a bit less than pristine.

CAR OWNERSHIP COSTS

CATEGORY	VARIABLES	ANNUAL COST
Fuel	15,000 miles per year ÷ 20 mpg x $2.50/gal	$1,875 per year or $156.25 per month
Insurance	[Town]	$100 per month
Maintenance/Repair	–	$100 per month
Depreciation	–	$250 per month

So, if the largest component of cost in owning and operating a motor vehicle is depreciation, is there a way to lower or reduce depreciation costs? Actually, there are two ways.

First, keep the vehicle for its full service life, meaning until it reaches approximately 12–15 years of age with more than 150,000 miles on the odometer. At this point in the vehicle's life—whether or not it still provides safe, reliable transportation—it's pretty well fully depreciated. Its value is less than $2,500, just one-tenth of its original price. From this point on, even if you continue to drive it, it's not going to depreciate much more unless it suffers a catastrophic mechanical failure, is destroyed in a crash, or is rusted or damaged to the point of having only salvage value.

Now, look again at the depreciation numbers. In this scenario, the total cost of ownership of that $25,000 new vehicle is $22,500 spread over 15 years. That's $1,500 per year, $125 per month, or a little over $30 per week—roughly one-half the monthly cost of ownership of the same vehicle purchased new and then sold or traded after five years. The equation is even more dramatic when you consider the initial three-years of ownership. The greatest dollar amount of depreciation occurs in the first few years you own and drive the vehicle. So, buying new and keeping the vehicle for its entire reliable service life is the number one way to keep the cost of ownership down. The second way is to buy a used car. No question, buying and driving a pre-owned motor vehicle can save you an enormous amount of money.

Again, do the math. If you purchase that same vehicle for $10,000 when it's five years old with 60,000 miles on the odometer, then drive it for the next 10 years and put 100,000-plus miles on it, it will be worth $2,500 or less, as illustrated in the previous scenario. Now, the total depreciation of $7,500 over 10 years, which works out to $750 per year, or a little over $60 per month—roughly one-fourth of the monthly cost for the same car if purchased new.

But of course, buying a used car adds measurable risk to the equation. The original factory warranty has been used up, and you likely won't know all the previous history on the vehicle, who owned it, how it was driven/used, what kind of maintenance it had, or any major mechanical failures or crashes in which it was involved.

If you like the idea of saving huge dollars in car ownership but are concerned about your increased vulnerability to unknown issues with a used vehicle, protect yourself. It's amazingly simple. Have the vehicle completely inspected—typically a $50–$100 service—by a professional independent third party. A shop or dealership with no vested interest in the vehicle will do a thorough inspection of the entire vehicle and give you a written report on its findings. This should identify any known issues with the vehicle and avoid those dreaded hidden surprises that don't surface until after you've signed on the dotted line. Check the *Yellow Pages* or call dealers and independent shops in your area for the availability and price of this service.

If there's any question about whether the vehicle has ever been seriously crashed, a body shop can do a similar inspection of the body, chassis, and paint. And you can do a simple inexpensive Carfax search via the internet, using the vehicle identification number (VIN) number of the car to determine the title and major repair history of the vehicle (www.carfax.com).

No, you cannot completely eliminate the inherent risks in buying a pre-owned motor vehicle, but you can certainly minimize them. Also, it's important to remember that there are literally thousands of good used cars and trucks available at any moment in time, so taking your time to find, test drive, and have the right vehicle inspected will also help reduce the risk and increase your comfort with buying a used car or truck.

To address the remaining risk, if the vehicle is new enough and low enough mileage, you may be able to purchase an extended warranty to cover the vehicle out to 6–10 years and 100,000 miles. Check carefully, though, to make sure any warranty of this type—which is actually more of a mechanical insurance policy—covers the vehicle bumper-to-bumper, and fits your annual driving mileage so that you will benefit from the coverage for as long as possible.

And finally, remember your monthly savings in depreciation for purchasing a used rather than new vehicle? By keeping about $200 per month in your pocket in savings, you've got a nice little nest egg for unexpected repairs. Even if you end up spending an unexpected $1,000 in repairs in the first of the 10 years you plan to own the vehicle, that only adds $100 per year, or less than $10 per month, to the cost of ownership.

BASIC MAINTENANCE SCHEDULE

The carmaker who designed, engineered, and built that fine automobile you drive every day has already provided you with a detailed schedule of required maintenance to keep your car or truck running strong for 150,000 miles or more; it's outlined in your owner's manual.

But how much of that is really essential to overall reliability and durability? How much of the work can you do yourself versus how much has to be done by a professional? Can the professional service be done by an independent shop, or does it have to be done by the car dealer?

Based on decades of experience and fleets of vehicles owned and maintained, following is a basic maintenance schedule for the essentials—those maintenance services that really are necessary for your vehicle to provide full service life. Will your car break or fail if you don't follow this schedule and/or do these services? Not necessarily. There are tens of thousands of very lucky car owners out there who live in blissful ignorance and continue to drive their vehicle well beyond recommended maintenance intervals . . . at least until something fails and leaves them stranded on the side of the road, frustrated and very angry at the vehicle for failing them.

Is the reverse also true? Yes, at times. Even with the absolutely best maintenance program, cars break. Engines fail, transmissions break, and radiators and air conditioning compressors seize. That's part of the risk of car ownership.

But there is absolutely no doubt that if you do, or have done, the basic maintenance necessary for your vehicle's survival, the percentages are on your side. In addition to routine engine oil and filter changes every 3,000–5,000 miles, make sure the second echelon of maintenance is done every three to five years or every 50,000 miles. This includes cooling system flush and refill, transmission fluid and filter service, brake fluid exchange, and changing the gear oil in the differential. These are the maintenance items that can make the difference between a vehicle delivering 150,000 miles without a major failure, and one that leaves its owner stranded on the side of the road with a $3,000 repair bill. Pay your money and take your choice. ■

MAINTENANCE SCHEDULE

TASK	SHOP COST	DIY COST	REASON TO DO	PROJECT NO. & PAGE
3,000–5,000 Miles/Twice per Year CHANGE ENGINE OIL AND FILTER	$25–$50	$15–$25	Engine longevity	Project 5: Change Oil and Filter
BASIC MAINTENANCE INSPECTION—INSPECT HOSES, BELTS, BRAKES, ALL FLUID LEVELS, WIPER BLADES, AND LIGHTING SYSTEM AT EVERY OIL CHANGE	No charge at better shops	No charge	Monitor condition of key components	
CHECK BRAKES AT EVERY OIL CHANGE	No charge at better shops	No charge	Maintain safe braking, avoid costly damage to rotors and drums	
CHECK TIRES/ TIRE PRESSURES/TREAD DEPTH MONTHLY; ROTATE TIRES EVERY 6,000–8,000 MILES	$20–$50	No charge	Maximize tire tread life and safety	Project 39: Check Tire Pressure; Project 40: Assess Tire Wear; Project 42: Rotate Tires
15,000 Miles/Annually CHANGE AIR FILTER, PCV VALVE FILTER, WIPER BLADES	$50–$100	$25–$40	Engine longevity, fuel mileage, visibility in inclement weather	Project 6: Change Air Filter; Project 7: Change PCV Valve

SEVERE SERVICE:
    Change transmission and transfer case fluid change differential fluid change fuel filter if recommended by carmaker.
    Inspect/clean/tighten battery cables and connections.
    Spray door/hood/trunk/hatch hinges/latches with aerosol lubricant.
	$250–$500	$50–$100	Extend service life of your car; particularly important if your vehicle sees severe service (extreme temperatures, lots of stops and starts, off-road use, etc.)	Project 3;
				Projects 31–36;
				Projects 14–15

30,000–50,000 Miles/3 Years CHANGE TRANSMISSION FLUID AND FILTER	$75–$150	$35–$50	Extend service life	Project 34–35
CHANGE DIFFERENTIAL FLUID	$20–$40	$10–$20	Extend service life	Project 32: Change Differential Fluid
CHANGE TRANSFER CASE OIL	$30–$60	$10–$20	Extend service life	
CHANGE BRAKE FLUID	$50–$100	$10–$20	Maintain proper function, avoid coorosion, frozen/rusted parts	Project 46: Bleed System
CHANGE FUEL FILTER	$15–$50	$5–$15	Maintain proper fuel flow	Project 3: Change Fuel Filter

MAINTENANCE SCHEDULE

TASK	SHOP COST	DIY COST	REASON TO DO	PROJECT NO. & PAGE
CHANGE ENGINE COOLANT	$60–$100	$20–$30	Maintain proper coolant temperature; avoid rusted/clogged system/overheating	Project 28: Flush Cooling System
CHANGE CABIN FILTER	$20–$40	$10–$20	Keep clean airflow into cabin	
REMOVE SPARK PLUGS TO INSPECT, REINSTALL WITH ANTI-SEIZE	$50–$100	$20–$50	Monitor engine/ ignition performance, condition of spark plug, prevent plug from seizing in cylinder head	Project 9: Change Plug Wires and Plugs
60,000–100,000 Miles/4–6 Years REPLACE COOLING SYSTEM HOSES	$100–$200	$20–$50	Avoid breakdown	Project 26: Replace Radiator Hose
REPLACE SERPENTINE BELT	$50–$150	$30–$50	Avoid breakdown	Project 8: Replace Serpentine Belt
REPLACE RADIATOR CAP	$10–$25	$2–$10	Maintain proper cooling system pressure	Project 25: Change Radiator Cap and Thermostat
REPLACE THERMOSTAT	$50–$150	$10–$20	Ensure proper engine temp	Project 25: Change Radiator Cap and Thermostat
REPLACE SPARK PLUGS	$50–$100	$10–$50	Improve combustion/ efficiency/mileage/ performance	Project 9: Change Plug Wires and Plugs
INSPECT SPARK PLUG WIRES	$100-$200	$50–$100	Replace worn/ damaged components, reducing inefficiency	
CHECK/REPLACE TIMING BELT (see owner's manual for suggested mileage)	$200–$400	$15–$40	Avoid breakdown, potential engine damage	

Project 1
Change Wiper Blades

TALENT: 1

TIME: 15 minutes

TOOLS: None, or a nail or small
          screwdriver depending on
          style of blade

COST: $15–$30

TIP: Set new blades next to old
          ones and determine
          mounting method and
          orientation before
          removing old blades.

1 When your wipers are not clearing the windshield cleanly during a rainstorm or when you use the washer, it's time for a new set. Changing them is an easy home project. Wiper arms are hinged near the base.

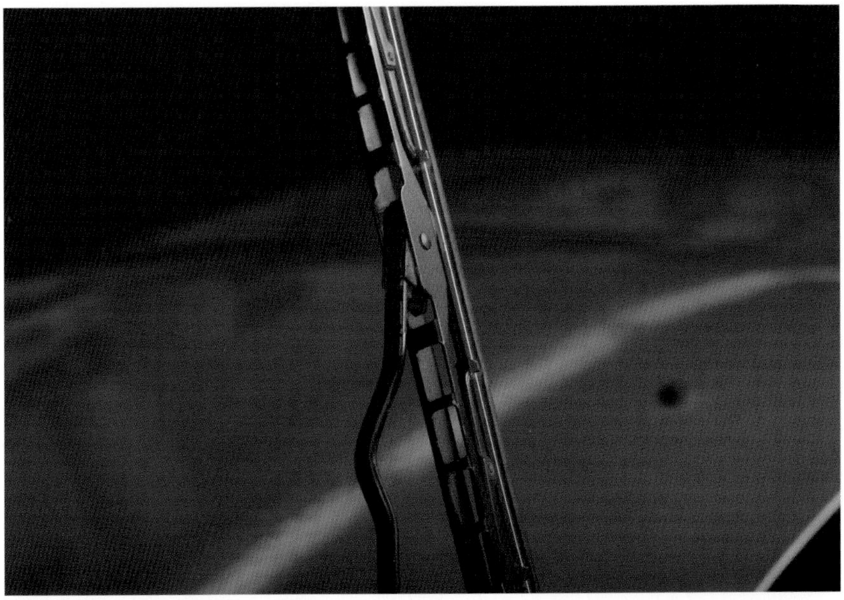

2 Most of these hinges allow you to lift the blade about perpendicular to the windshield, where it will stay. If not, you need to hold it up as you remove the blade.

3 This common style uses a U-shaped clip that you compress to remove the blade. Find the little button inside the U and push it toward the other end of the clip. Another style attaches to a small, grooved shaft gripped by a spring clip. This style has a hole marked "push." You insert a thin object, like a nail, into the hole to release the clip and slide off the blade. The new blade clicks over the shaft.

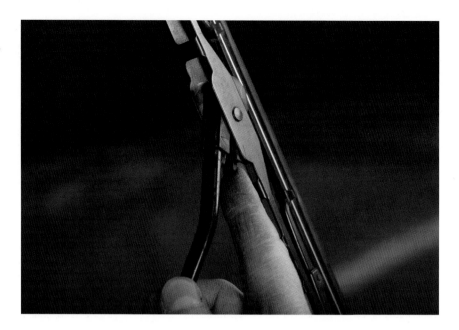

4 With the U-clip compressed as shown above, slide the wiper blade toward the base of the arm, which will cause the arm's U-shaped end to pull free of the clip. (Doing this will likely push the rubber blade out a bit.) Shift the arm end so that it clears the clip and passes out a hole above it, freeing the blade. To put the new one on, reverse the directions just given.

Project 2
Fill
Washer Fluid

TALENT:	1
TIME:	5 minutes
TOOLS:	Washer fluid
COST:	$2
TIP:	Use care when opening and closing the cap in cold weather, as thin ones can become brittle and crack.

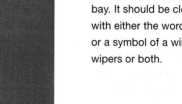

1 The fluid reservoir is in the engine bay. It should be clearly marked with either the words "washer fluid" or a symbol of a windshield and wipers or both.

2 Lift the cap, fill the bottle with washer fluid, and close. Washer fluid is not stored under pressure, so it does not have the exacting fill standards as other fluids. Typical fill level is just below the cap.

FILL WASHER FLUID

How To Jack Up Your Car

1 The jack that comes with your car is for changing tires only. Never work on your vehicle while any part of it is supported by this jack—it is absolutely not safe. The vehicle should be level and safely supported on jack stands, or with the front tires driven up and parked on metal ramps.

Most, if not all, of today's cars do not have a separate chassis or frame. Instead, the body and chassis are combined in a unibody construction. You must take care in jacking a new vehicle to avoid damaging it. The owner's or shop manual will identify the places underneath the vehicle where it is safe to place a jack. If you are not sure, ask a qualified mechanic for your make and model vehicle.

2 This Honda has a front crossmember that is strong enough to support the front end's weight. We placed a floor jack in the center of this crossmember and raised the vehicle high enough to place jack stands on either side. The jack stands are placed on frame-like members close to the engine compartment in front. Be absolutely sure you place the jack and the jack stands in a spot capable of taking the weight.

3 We placed the rear axle stands in the same spot designated to jack up the vehicle for a tire change. This is the spot designated by the manufacturer.

With the car properly placed on jack stands, there is plenty of room to work underneath in comfort and safety.

How To Clean Your Hands

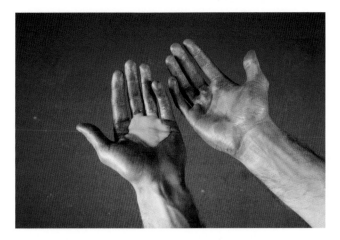

1 Some people steer clear of auto repairs just because of the dirt and grease. Fortunately, new auto-specific hand cleaners remove all the grease, grime, and oil. Apply a good dollop of an auto-grade hand cleaner in the palm of your hand.

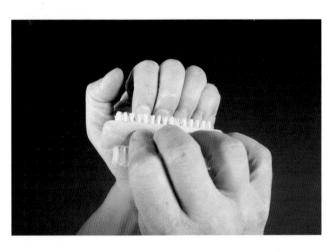

2 Work it in well, not just to the front and back but in the knuckles and fingertips too.

3 A stiff fingernail brush will get that grease out so none of your officemates know you've been productive in the garage over the weekend.

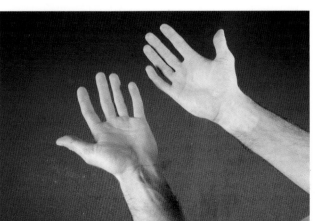

4 These are the same hands after the hand cleaner. Look near the wrists where the cleaner wasn't applied. Hands perfectly clean and ready for paperwork or a nice restaurant.

Chapter 2
Fuel System

☠ WARNING!	⚠ KEY CONCEPT
📯 OLD SCHOOL TECH	🔧 MAINTENANCE TIP
🛸 TOMORROW'S TECH	🐷 MONEY-SAVING TIP

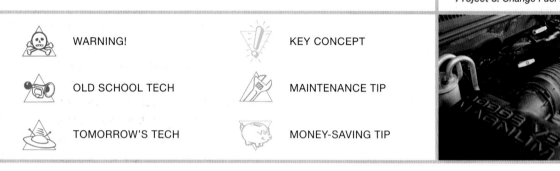

How far can you drive your vehicle once it's out of fuel? This is a rhetorical question, obviously, and a reminder that it is the energy in the fuel that ultimately provides the power to move the vehicle. When your car runs raggedly, stalls, or refuses to start, a problem with the fuel system is a likely culprit. Ignition, or lack of spark, is the other most likely problem, but that's explained later in Chapter 4, Electrical System.

The process is not quite as simple as pouring gasoline into the engine, although this technique was used in some of the earliest engines. Gasoline must first be atomized, then vaporized, then mixed with air; only then can it be burned to produce power.

So how is the fuel processed so that it's ready to burn in the engine? That's the definition of the vehicle's fuel system. Perhaps the simplest way to understand the fuel system in your automobile is to identify its three main functions: storage, transportation, and delivery.

When you stop by the self-service gas station, stick the automatic dispensing nozzle into the fuel filler opening on your vehicle, and squeeze the handle, you are starting the fuel on the last leg of its long journey—from oil fields somewhere in the world, a trip across the big sea in a huge tanker, piped underground to a refining plant, trucked to the gas station, stored in

an underground tank, and finally pumped into the fuel tank on your vehicle—whew! And all this for a product that still costs less than bottled water!

When you fill your tank, you're safely storing enough fuel to drive your vehicle roughly 300–500 miles. The tank itself is a steel or plastic container strapped to the chassis of the vehicle in a protected location, fitted with internal baffles to prevent sloshing and spillage, and plumbed to deliver the fuel to the engine via a fuel pump and fuel lines. The tank is effectively sealed once the filler cap is properly tightened, not just to prevent spillage but to prevent fuel vapors from escaping into the atmosphere.

Modern motor vehicles feature evaporative emission systems to prevent the loss of fuel vapor—unburned hydrocarbons—into the atmosphere, creating pollution. The entire fuel system is sealed and electronically monitored so that any loss of pressure or vacuum in the tank—such as would occur if you refueled your vehicle with the engine running (a big no-no)—will trigger the check engine light, requiring a trip to the shop to reset the light, an inconvenience and expense that will remind you to shut the engine off during refueling.

The vapors generated by the gasoline in the tank are stored in the tank and its fuel separator, effectively a small tank within the tank perforated with small holes to slow the filling process. This little tank is not intended to fill with fuel during refueling—that's why you don't want to keep clicking the fuel nozzle repeatedly until you've forced the last possible ounce of fuel into the tank.

The vapors are collected in the charcoal canister in the engine compartment, which stores them until the engine is started. The purge valve, controlled by the vehicle's engine management computer, opens a valve to apply engine manifold vacuum to the canister to draw these vapors into the induction system and burn them as the vehicle initially warms up. The idea is to completely consume the fuel vapors to prevent unburned fuel from escaping into the atmosphere.

How serious is the effort to control fuel vapors in modern automobiles? If you're a Californian, you'll instantly recognize the unique vapor recovery bellows on fuel dispensing nozzles on the pumps at gas stations.

All right, the tank's full, the filler cap is secure, and you're ready to start the engine. In automotive decades before fuel injection, the fuel pump that moved fuel from the tank to the engine was mechanical. It was mounted on the side of the engine and operated by an egg-shaped lobe on the camshaft. The pump featured a rubber diaphragm that cycled up and down inside a chamber, creating a vacuum—actually, a pressure differential—that drew or sucked the fuel from the tank through the fuel line to the pump. From the pump, the fuel was pushed through a filter and into the carburetor.

Modern cars use electric fuel pumps built into the gas tank (more on those pumps can be found under the heading Fuel Injection).

Note: **You can skip the carburetor section if you have a newer car with fuel injection.**

CARBURETORS

Carburetors (may they rest in peace in that big automotive heaven in the sky) were devices that helped the fuel transition from its liquid state into smaller atomized particles, which vaporized and mixed with the incoming air drawn into the engine by the downward motion of the pistons. It is this vaporized air/fuel mixture which the engine then burns to make power.

Carburetors feature a number of different circuits to help them do the complete job. As the fuel enters the carburetor from the fuel line, it fills the float chamber or bowl—a small reservoir of fuel in the carburetor body. The flow of fuel into this chamber is metered by a simple needle and seat valve operated by a mechanical float arm. As the fuel level in the chamber rises or falls, it progressively closes or opens the valve, regulating the level of fuel in the chamber and available to the engine.

The choke circuit restricts the flow of air through the carburetor, thus increasing the percentage of fuel mixed with that air and providing a richer air/fuel mixture to help the engine start and warm up. You can actually see this by removing the top of the air cleaner assembly, pushing the throttle once to set the choke, and watching the choke air valve close on the top of the carburetor. As the engine starts, the choke pull-off, operated by engine vacuum, pulls against the tension of the choke spring to progressively re-open the choke air valve as the engine warms up. If all these parts are well synchronized, the engine starts cleanly and runs smoothly through the warm-up period. If they are not, the engine floods easily on a cold start—too much choke for too long—or bucks and hesitates when you try to apply power—too little choke for too short a time period.

The most unique feature of a carburetor is its venturi, based on the aerodynamic principle of the venturi effect. When atmospheric air is drawn through an opening into a chamber of increasing volume, its pressure decreases. The throttle plate, connected to the throttle pedal under your right foot, varies the venturi opening, which controls the volume of air being drawn into the engine. At idle with your foot off the pedal, the throttle is almost closed, restricting airflow into the engine. At full throttle when you're trying to safely enter the freeway before the semi cuts you off, airflow into the engine is maximized.

Remember the fuel waiting in the float bowl? It is under normal atmospheric pressure. The main jets are small tubes or orifices that connect the bottom of the float chamber to the venturi. As the throttle is opened and closed, the pressure differential between the float chamber and venturi meters the amount of fuel pushed from the float through the jets into the air stream drawn through the venturi. By varying the volume of air and amount of fuel drawn into the engine from the carburetor, you regulate the power produced by your car.

Many carburetors also feature an accelerator pump, which mechanically squirts a little extra fuel into the

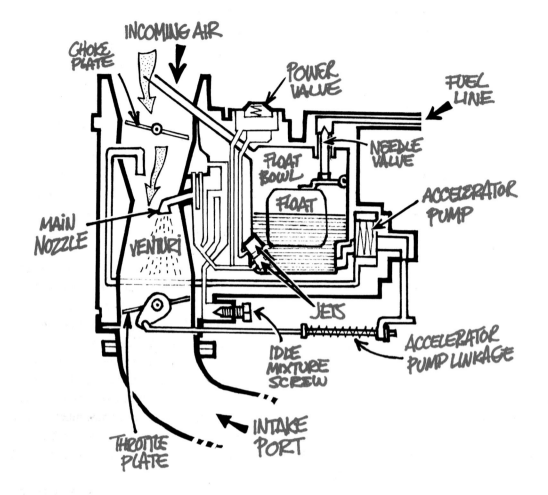

venturi as you step on the throttle. The movement of the throttle activates this little pump, which helps the engine begin accelerating cleanly and without bogging.

For the first eight decades of the automobile, carburetors were the device of choice to regulate and mix fuel with the incoming air. And carburetors did a fine job of this in most cases. They were relatively easy to tune by varying the size of the main jets, for example, and when tuned well, they provided good performance and fuel economy.

CARBURETOR DRAWBACKS

To paraphrase Clint Eastwood, "every carburetor has its limitation," primarily the inability to recognize and accommodate changes in atmospheric air pressure. For example, a carburetor tuned properly for operation at sea level along the coast won't perform very well in the mountains. The higher the altitude, the lower the ambient air pressure, the fewer molecules of air per cubic foot. But the carburetor only knows how many cubic feet of air flows through it, thus the sea level carb will deliver too much fuel for the amount of air

pulled through it in the mountains, meaning the engine will run too rich.

Carburetors have other drawbacks as well, particularly in controlling emissions of unburned hydrocarbons. External emission systems were added to the last generations of carburetors in an attempt to help them conform to the first generation of emissions requirements in the 1970s and early 1980s. These add-on devices were somewhat successful, but overly complex, extremely annoying, and often caused drivability issues with the vehicle.

FUEL INJECTION

Cars built since about 1980 use fuel injection to deliver fuel to the engine. Compared to a carburetor, fuel injection provides improved performance and fuel economy, and reduces emissions. Why does fuel injection work so well? In simple terms, fuel injectors do a better job of controlling precisely how much fuel is metered into the engine, and a much better job of atomizing the fuel, making it easier to vaporize and burn.

Fuel injection works by pushing fuel under significant mechanical pressure into the air stream drawn into the engine. This higher pressure breaks up—or atomizes—the fuel into smaller droplets, which then vaporize better in the low-pressure air (vacuum) flowing into the engine. This helps the fuel vapor mix with the air and burn more efficiently.

Early fuel injection systems were mechanical in nature, often timed and driven (like the ignition) off the camshaft. A high-pressure pump was timed to deliver fuel under pressure into the induction system. The injectors themselves were also mechanical in nature, utilizing a spring-loaded ball to seal the end of the injector nozzle in most cases. When fuel pressure increased above the resistance of the spring, the ball was forced off the seat of the injector and fuel sprayed into the engine. As the pressure dropped, the ball closed the injector and stopped the flow of fuel.

ELECTRONIC FUEL INJECTION (EFI)

Starting in the late 1970s and early 1980s, carmakers have moved on to electronic fuel injection (EFI) systems, which offer a number of practical advantages. EFI is simpler, requires fewer components, and as such is more reliable and durable. But more importantly, electronic fuel injection systems are completely controlled by computers. That means the computer can be programmed, or mapped, to provide exactly the correct amount of fuel to each cylinder in virtually every possible driving situation. The increase in efficiency, performance, drivability, and fuel mileage,

coupled with the reduction in emissions, has crowned EFI as king of fuel delivery, leaving carburetors as relics of an earlier automotive era.

Electronic fuel injection is deceptively simple. The fuel pump for these systems is now mounted near or inside the fuel tank for two reasons. First, to deliver fuel at much higher pressures, often 40–80 psi; it's mechanically easier to push rather than pull the fuel. Second, the tank-mounted pump is far less prone to engine compartment heat and the dreaded vapor-lock syndrome—where the fuel boils somewhere close to the engine, causing a loss of pressure and big drivability issues.

The pump draws fuel through a fine screen in the tank, then pushes the fuel under significant pressure through a large fuel filter and forward to the injection system in the engine compartment. In a throttle-body injection system, the fuel is delivered to one or more fuel injectors mounted in a venturi-shaped throttle body, which somewhat resembles a carburetor. The computer regulates the precise amount of time the injector is open, thus accurately controlling how much fuel is sprayed into the venturi, where it mixes with the incoming air and is delivered via the intake manifold to each cylinder.

In a port injection system, the fuel is delivered to the fuel rail mounted along the intake manifold, which feeds individual injectors for each cylinder.

FUEL INJECTION SYSTEM

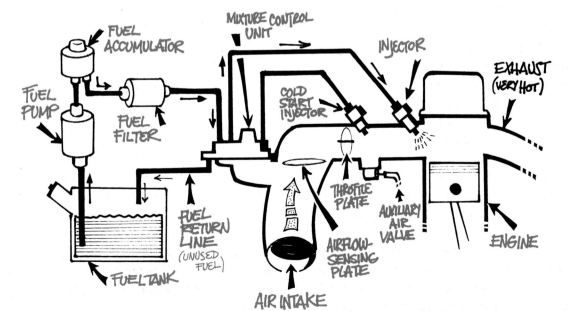

The injectors are mounted in the intake manifold or cylinder head, aimed directly at the intake valve. They are timed to spray an exact amount of well-atomized fuel directly into the airflow entering the cylinder through the intake valve. The primary advantage of port injection is an injector for every cylinder, which provides extremely accurate fuel metering.

A typical port injector is a simple electromagnetic solenoid, which when energized by a pulse-width signal from the engine management computer, pulls a pintle off its seat, opening the injector for a specific period of time (measured in milliseconds), delivering a very precise, very finely atomized spray of fuel.

Carmakers have also fitted high-pressure flapper-valve injection systems to vehicles that feature a flapper valve, which feeds high pressure fuel to a mechanical poppet-style injector for each cylinder.

Automakers are also working with direct fuel injection systems that, as the name implies, inject fuel under high pressure directly into the combustion chamber. All of these efforts are engineered to improve the efficiency of combustion, increasing fuel economy and power, and reducing emissions.

Fuel pressure in an EFI system is controlled by a fuel pressure regulator. In most cases, this device is mounted at the end of the fuel rail or fuel path through the throttle body, and regulates the percentage of fuel returned to the fuel tank. By varying that percentage, the system can raise or lower fuel pressure to trim the amount of fuel delivered to the engine. Most fuel pressure regulators operate off engine vacuum. When engine vacuum falls as the throttle is opened, less fuel is redirected to the fuel tank, thus increasing fuel pressure available at the injectors and delivering a bit more fuel during the injector's pulse width (the precise amount of time it's open), richening the mixture for acceleration. At cruise speed, engine vacuum is high, which reduces fuel pressure, delivering a bit less fuel as the injector opens and helping to optimize fuel economy.

ENGINE MANAGEMENT SYSTEM

Okay, now we know how the fuel is delivered to the injectors, but what controls how long each injector stays open and how much fuel is sprayed into the engine? That's the job of the engine management system. Modern motor vehicles feature incredibly sophisticated, computer-controlled engine management systems with far more computing power than the systems on early spacecraft, believe it or not. A series of sensors provides information to the computer, which then calculates the amount of fuel necessary for that instant in time, and commands the injectors to open for a specific amount of time to deliver precisely that amount of fuel. It repeats this process for each injection pulse and monitors the sensor inputs hundreds of times per second. Pretty amazing, eh?

Basic inputs to the computer include coolant temperature, engine speed, crankshaft position,

TYPES OF FUEL INJECTION SYSTEMS

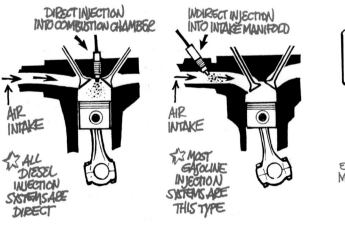

DIRECT INJECTION INTO COMBUSTION CHAMBER

INDIRECT INJECTION INTO INTAKE MANIFOLD

AIR INTAKE

AIR INTAKE

☆ ALL DIESEL INJECTION SYSTEMS ARE DIRECT

☆ MOST GASOLINE INJECTION SYSTEMS ARE THIS TYPE

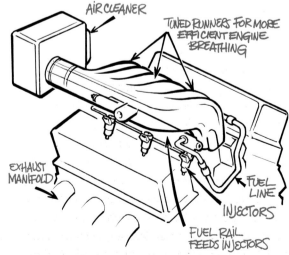

AIR CLEANER

TUNED RUNNERS FOR MORE EFFICIENT ENGINE BREATHING

EXHAUST MANIFOLD

FUEL LINE

INJECTORS

FUEL RAIL FEEDS INJECTORS

throttle position, manifold pressure, and incoming air temperature. The computer's program monitors these and computes the injector pulse width—the amount of time the injector stays open in that combustion cycle. Once the engine is warmed up, this pulse width is trimmed, or finely tuned, by the signal from the oxygen sensor in the exhaust. This critical little device compares the percentage of oxygen in the exhaust gases coming from the engine with the percentage of oxygen in the atmosphere. Then it generates an electrical voltage signal based on this difference and communicates this to the computer many times per second, which helps the EFI system adjust air/fuel mixtures as close to perfect—the ideal 14.7 to 1 air/fuel ratio—as possible.

Can you see how EFI systems are inherently so much more efficient than any carburetor?

ENGINE MANAGEMENT SYSTEM

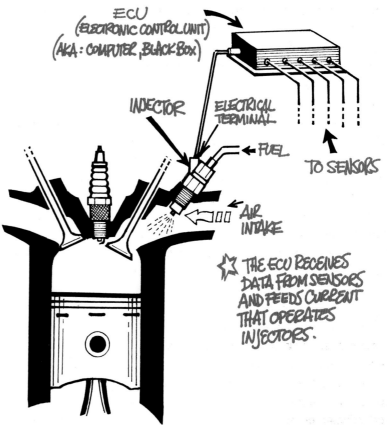

ECU
(ELECTRONIC CONTROL UNIT)
(AKA: COMPUTER, BLACK BOX)

INJECTOR

ELECTRICAL TERMINAL

← FUEL

TO SENSORS

AIR INTAKE

☆ THE ECU RECEIVES DATA FROM SENSORS AND FEEDS CURRENT THAT OPERATES INJECTORS.

TAKING CARE OF THE FUEL SYSTEM

Basic maintenance of fuel systems involves two "Fs": filters and fuel. It was important to replace the fuel filter on carbureted engines periodically so that they didn't pack up with debris and stop flowing fuel. Sintered metallic filters mounted right at the carburetor's fuel inlet were somewhat prone to this. Interestingly, most carbureted engines didn't have fuel filters between the fuel tank and fuel pump.

Fuel Filter Changes

Fuel filters on fuel injected engines are even more critical. These filters are typically quite large in size and volume, and are mounted in, at, or close to the fuel tank itself. The fuel filter traps debris, crud, and even water from the fuel, and should be change at least every 30,000 miles. If the filter begins to clog, its resistance to fuel flow increases, which works the electric fuel pump in the tank much harder. A $15 fuel filter is a much simpler, less expensive service than $500–$800 to replace the fuel pump itself. And of course, a clogged fuel filter or failed fuel pump will

absolutely, positively leave you and your vehicle dead on the side of the road until the problem is fixed. You can't limp a fuel injected vehicle with a clogged fuel system; the engine will not run.

One extremely important service note when replacing fuel filters. On a carbureted engine, some minor fuel spillage can occur when the fuel line is disconnected to change the filter. But remember, fuel injected engines operate at very high fuel pressures. Opening or disconnecting any fuel system component without fully depressurizing the system is extremely dangerous. Many fuel filters require a special tool to disconnect the fuel lines. That's why changing the fuel filter on modern EFI systems is best left to an automotive professional.

Air Filter Changes

One more filter to service on a regular basis: the air filter. Keep it simple: change the air filter once a year. If you live or drive in a dusty environment or on dirt roads, change the air filter more frequently, perhaps every six months.

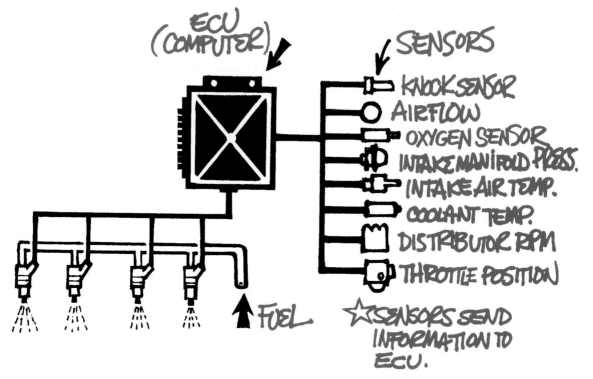

Any serious restriction of airflow through the air filter will significantly decrease the fuel mileage from your vehicle. This restriction will literally strangle your engine.

But why filter the air at all? To clean it, of course. Well, the filter doesn't really clean the air itself, it's designed to remove fine particles, dirt, and debris from the air before they are ingested by the engine. Any type of debris entering the engine acts like sandpaper on cylinder walls, increasing the rate of wear on pistons, rings, and cylinder walls, and shortening their lives and the life of the engine. This is never a good thing, so make sure the air induction system components are well sealed, and change the air filter regularly.

Choose the Proper Fuel

The other F in fuel system maintenance is the fuel itself. For gasoline engines, your first concern is to use the correct octane fuel for your vehicle. Here's the rule of thumb: *Use the lowest octane fuel your vehicle's engine will operate on satisfactorily.* The corollary is this: *There is no advantage to using fuel with an octane rating higher than the engine requires. None!* With the price of gasoline continuing to climb, that's a worthwhile piece of information.

The vast majority of motor vehicles operate perfectly satisfactorily on regular unleaded, which carries an average octane rating of 86–88 octane. Some higher performance, power, and priced vehicles call for premium octane fuels, typically in the 91–93 octane range. Many, if not most, of these can operate satisfactorily on 89–90 octane mid-grade fuels, if not on 87 octane regular. Why? Knock sensors.

The knock sensor provides another input to the engine management computer to help it determine the precise air/fuel mixture and spark timing for the engine. The sensor is literally a small microphone that's tuned to hear the unique sounds of engine knock or ping—detonation or pre-ignition caused by inadequate octane fuel. In most cases, pinging sounds like a handful of small pebbles in a tin can and is most often heard up to light to moderate acceleration. If and when the knock sensor hears this, the computer is programmed to richen the air/fuel mixture and/or retard engine timing, both of which will lower combustion temperatures to prevent knock and potential engine damage.

Pre-Ignition and Detonation

Visualize lighting the corner of a piece of paper with a match and watching the flame front spread across and consume the paper—that's exactly what is supposed to happen in the combustion chamber, only much, much faster.

Pre-ignition and/or detonation can occur when residual temperatures in the combustion chamber reach the point where the fuel will being to ignite on its own, without the benefit of a spark. If this occurs before the point at which the spark plug fires, it's called pre-ignition and creates a dry rattling sound (it literally sounds like something is knocking or tapping on your engine wall). That means the cylinder isn't burning the air/fuel mixture efficiently. This phenomenon is also called knocking or pinging and it robs the engine of power and generates excess combustion chamber heat. Ultimately, pre-ignition can actually melt or burn a hole in a piston or burn the edge of a valve.

Pre-ignition can lead to detonation, which occurs when hot spots in the combustion chamber—due to heat and pressure—start the fire burning in those areas while the spark plug starts the fire in another. When the flame fronts meet, they create and audible knock that can be very destructive to pistons. The extraordinarily high pressures developed by detonation can actually hammer a hole in a piston.

All of today's fuels are unleaded, meaning they no longer contain tetraethyl lead. For decades, lead was added to fuel as an inexpensive way to increase octane rating and lubricate exhaust valves and valve seats. The concept of lubricating valve seats really addressed the efficiency of heat transfer from the valve to the valve seat during the period the valve was closed. Lead additives helped facilitate that transfer.

Since approximately 1970, carmakers have utilized hardened or sodium-filled exhaust valves and hardened valve seat inserts to deal with this heat issue. So we don't need the lead for this purpose anymore. If you drive an older vehicle (way older!) or a collector vehicle with a pre-1970 engine,

TOP TEN FUEL/GAS SAVING TIPS

With gas and diesel fuel prices way up and continuing to climb, it's worth paying attention to what you drive, when you drive, where you drive, and how you drive.

Here are my top ten tips for saving fuel:

1. **Drive less.** The best way to save fuel is to not burn it. Consolidate trips, car pool when possible, and drive during off-peak hours to avoid congestion.

2. **Drive slower,** perhaps the speed limit for a change? At freeway speeds, aerodynamics play a measurable role in fuel economy. Driving in the 60–65-mile-per-hour range instead of 75-plus miles per hour will likely increase your fuel mileage by 2 or more miles per gallon.

3. **Keep the engine in tune.** What does that mean with today's electronically fuel-injected engines? Not much, other than making sure the engine is running as it should. Spark plugs, air filters, and oxygen sensors are the primary components that influence fuel economy. Install a new air filter once per year—or more frequently if

you live/drive on dirt/dusty roads—and have the engine scoped on an engine analyzer every 30,000–50,000 miles to make sure it's running properly.

4. **Properly inflate your tires.** Pressures at or above 30–35 psi are a good choice for most passenger cars. At higher inflation pressures, the tire's rolling resistance decreases—it takes less power to roll the tires down the road. That saves you fuel.

5. **Keep tires/wheels properly aligned.** Not only will this help tires last longer, but properly aligned tires offer less rolling resistance, thus, slightly better fuel mileage.

6. **Keep the front of vehicle clean and free of debris,** especially in the grille opening. Keeping the air conditioning condenser and radiator free of bugs, leaves, and debris allows the engine to cool more efficiently and the air conditioning to work less to keep occupants cool—both of which will save fuel.

7. **Accelerate modestly.** It takes fuel to make power, so the harder you accelerate, the more fuel the engine burns. At freeway speed, accelerate gently to avoid transmission

downshifts if possible. Again, lower engine rpm generally means less fuel consumption.

8. **Coast as much and as often as you can.** Anticipate stop signs, traffic lights, and slowdowns. Why keep accelerating toward a stop? Lifting off the throttle and coasting toward the stop or slowdown obviously saves fuel.

9. **Brake gently and as little as possible**—within reason, of course; you still need to stop before the intersection. Applying your brakes converts energy from fuel you've already burned accelerating the vehicle back into heat. Don't waste what you've already spent; coast as much as possible and brake as little as possible.

10. **Eyes up!** Look as far ahead as possible to maintain good situational awareness. The farther ahead you look, the more time and distance you have to adjust the speed and direction of your vehicle. Good situational awareness is the key to safe driving, and it also saves fuel by helping you anticipate the need to slow or stop early, allowing you to do so gently and progressively.

you'll find a number of lead substitutes at auto parts stores to deal with the exhaust valve/seat issue. Use them periodically.

The federal government finally eliminated tetraethyl lead from motor fuels in the mid-1980s. With the increasing recognition of its toxicity and danger to humans, along with the technological advances in engine design and metallurgy, lead faded into automotive history.

Oxygenated Fuel

Today's motor fuels are still a blend of long-chain hydrocarbons, but often include a percentage of oxygenate to increase octane and reduce emissions and support our farm economy. The oxygenate of choice today is ethanol, an alcohol derived from grain, primarily corn. U.S. cities covered by federal clean-air legislation due to air pollution problems typically require oxygenated fuels during the winter season. Many states require oxygenated fuels year round, and their state and local requirements require specific blends of oxygenates. In a sense, they are designer fuels.

Most oxygenated fuels are a 10 percent blend of ethanol with 90 percent gasoline. For late model vehicles, this fuel operates seamlessly, providing good performance and reasonable mileage along with good emissions control. Some older vehicles don't particularly like these fuels and may deliver less mileage and drivability. Much older vehicles, roughly 1980 or older, may be prone to potential damage to fuel system components from these fuels. Aren't you glad you asked!

There is a price for using oxygenated fuels. By the very nature of alcohol compared to pure gasoline, ethanol contains just 50–60 percent of the actual BTU energy per gallon. Simple math tells us that a 10 percent ethanol blend should deliver approximately 5 percent less fuel mileage. That's the way it is, folks, live with it.

Looking at the other side of the equation, ethanol has an octane rating of about 115, meaning it helps raise the octane level of the gasoline with which it's mixed.

The good news is that modern automobiles are designed, engineered, and built to run on oxygenated fuels, so in day-to-day driving you will likely never notice the difference, except perhaps in that minor fuel mileage loss. Said differently, if you fill up your vehicle in a community that does not require oxygenated fuels, then fill up next time with oxygenated fuels, you likely won't notice any difference in startability, drivability, or performance.

But there is one characteristic of ethanol-blended fuels that can be an issue for car owners: the ethanol would rather mix with water than gasoline. The term is phase-separation and it means that the ethanol component of the fuel is bonding with the very small percentage of water that may be present in the fuel, creating a layer of gasoline and a layer of ethanol/water. If this happens, your engine will run very poorly, if at all.

To prevent this phase-separation, fuel suppliers add co-solvents to help keep the ethanol and gasoline mixed. They also try to prevent any water from contaminating the fuel during the refining, blending, and transportation of the fuel to the station. In fact, the ethanol component is only added to the tanker truck just before transportation to the gas station.

DEALING WITH FUEL IN COLD WEATHER

As a car owner, today it's an even better idea to keep the fuel tank as full as possible. Less air space in the fuel tank means less air and less moisture in the air that may condense into liquid form on the inside surfaces of the tank. Keeping the tank as full as possible during winter makes perfect sense, as does adding the occasional can of fuel system cleaner/de-moisturizer.

However, since most refiners add a small percentage of isopropyl alcohol to winter fuel blends to attract, mix with, and carry moisture through the fuel system, there's no need to add fuel system de-icing products on a regular basis. Don't think of these as "if a little is good, more is better." In fact, too much total alcohol in the fuel system can be a big problem.

Of interest in this equation is the fact that isopropyl alcohol, also known as wood alcohol, can actually help remix phase-separated ethanol/water with gasoline. That's why it works at de-icing the fuel system. ◼

PROBLEM	PROBABLE CAUSES	ACTION TO REPAIR
ENGINE CRANKS BUT WON'T START	No fuel pressure caused by the car being out of gas; fuel line blocked, broken, or disconnected; fuel pump not functioning	Start with **Fuel Pump Hum/Sound Test**
	Fuel Pump Hum/Sound Test	Turn on key, listen for fuel pump operation (a whine or hum that lasts for about 2 seconds). Fuel pump should run for two seconds, then stop
	If you hear fuel pump hum, fuel pump and fuel relay are working	Go to **Check Ignition Switch**
	If you don't hear hum, fuel pump is not working	Go to **Fuel Pump Relay Check**
NO FUEL PUMP OPERATION	**Fuel Pump Relay Check**	Locate fuel pump relay in relay panel; check owner's manual. Hold hand on relay as key is turned on. Feel for "click" as relay engages
	Relay does not click	Replace relay. DIY (fuel pump relays are available at auto parts stores) or take car to professional
	Relay clicks but fuel pump doesn't run	Have professional test the fuel pump for pressure/volume and possibly replace it
	Check Ignition Switch	Do dash warning lights illuminate when key is turned to "on," then go off as key is turned to "start"?
	Ignition switch tests bad	Replace ignition switch
	Ignition switch tests OK	Go to **Check Fuel Pump/ECM Fuse**
	Check Fuel Pump/ECM Fuse	Find fuse box (see your owner's manual); slots should be labeled. Remove fuse from fuel pump/ECM slot; replace with new fuse and turn ignition switch on and listen for fuel pump hum. Note that some new cars don't have the slots in fuse box labeled; check ALL the fuses on these cars. *(Project 17: Test and Replace Fuses)*
	Failed/open fuse	Replace fuse. *(Project 17: Test and Replace Fuses)*
	Fuse is OK	Go to **Check Impact/Rollover Circuit Breaker**
	Check Impact/Rollover Circuit Breaker	Check owner's manual for location, usually in trunk/luggage compartment
LONG CRANK TIME BEFORE ENGINE STARTS	Blocked fuel-tank vent creating vacuum	Remove fuel filler cap, try starting engine again
	Loss of fuel pressure preventing car from starting	Perform fuel pressure leakdown test. *(Project 30: Pressure Leakdown Test)*
	Fuel pressure drops in less than 10 minutes	Check fuel pressure regulator/vacuum line

FUEL SYSTEM

2

31

PROBLEM	PROBABLE CAUSES	ACTION TO REPAIR
	Vacuum line to regulator is wet with fuel	Replace regulator
	Vacuum line to regulator is dry	Go to **Check Fuel Injectors for Leakage**
	Check Fuel Injectors for Leakage	Check fuel pump/check valve/pulsator for leakage
	ECM/ignition switch problem, fuel pump isn't powered until engine builds oil pressure	Replace the ECM or ignition switch
POOR PERFORM-ANCE, ACCELERATION, IDLE QUALITY	Low fuel pressure	Check fuel pump for volume, pressure, and amperage draw
	Check idle air control and EGR valve	Check electrical/vacuum connections
	Quality and octane of gasoline	Try higher octane fuel
	Check with gas station to determine if problem is contaminated fuel	
MISFIRE/ENGINE ROUGHNESS	Injectors clogged	Add can of injector cleaner or have injector professionally cleaned
	Fuel filter clogged	Replace fuel filter. *(Project 3: Change Fuel Filter)*
RAW FUEL ODOR	Potential fuel leak	Check for evidence of fuel leak; inspect engine compartment, under car, near fuel tank.
		WARNING: If you smell gas, do not start or drive vehicle until problem is found
	Evaporative emission system problem with purge valve, fuel filler cap, charcoal canister	Have system inspected by repair shop

Project 3
Change Fuel Filter

TALENT: 2–3

TIME: 15–30 minutes

TOOLS: Screwdriver or spring-clip remover

COST: $10–$50

TIP: Use a rag over the fuel line fittings as you remove them to minimize spilled gas.

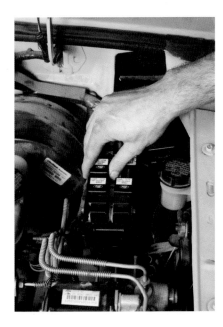

1 Garages have tools to depressurize a fuel injection system. You can accomplish this at home by removing the fuel pump relay, then turning the key repeatedly. The vehicle will not start, or will start only momentarily and stall. Either way, you reduce the fuel system pressure.

This will not completely depressurize the fuel system or completely eliminate fuel leakage when fuel lines are loosened or disconnected. Wrap a rag or shop towel around the connection to catch and soak up any spilled fuel.

2 Fuel filters are often on the chassis rail underneath the vehicle, as on this Ford Ranger truck. (The arrow points from the fuel tank toward the engine to show proper mounting orientation.)

Never use incandescent light sources or smoke when working on fuel systems. Use a sealed-beam flashlight instead.

3 Remove the filter from its bracket, which may be a clip or screw-down type or like this one from which the filter simply pulls free.

4 Remove the clip or clamp securing the hose.

5 Place a towel over the fitting to avoid spraying gas and pull the fuel line off the filter.

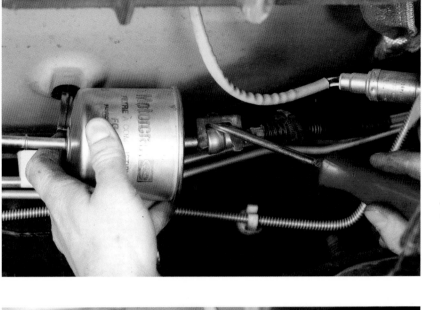

6 Remove the front clip.

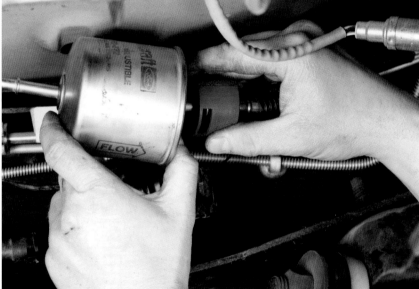

7 The front fitting uses a round spring clip that resides inside the fuel line where it connects to the filter. This type of fitting requires a special, inexpensive tool. Open the tool, fit it around the fuel line, and then press a collar inside the tool up into the fitting holding the spring clip. This releases the clip and allows you to pull the filter free.

Note: Some fuel filters reside in inconvenient places and may require a lot more work, such as disconnecting and lowering the fuel tank. If you buy the filter and find you are in over your head, stop before you disconnect any fittings. Any garage can change the filter for you. Your manual will tell you the service interval for filter replacement. Typically, it's 15,000–30,000 miles. To install the new filter, reverse the removal procedure.

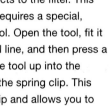

Chapter 3
Engine

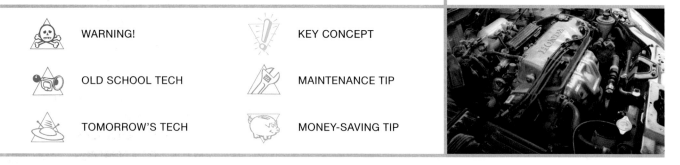

WARNING!

KEY CONCEPT

OLD SCHOOL TECH

MAINTENANCE TIP

TOMORROW'S TECH

MONEY-SAVING TIP

Identify the following: DOHC EFI 3.5L L5. Is it:

A. A new implantable medical device?
B. The latest is digital TV technology?
C. The Da Vinci Code?
D. The engine in Chevy's Colorado light truck?

If you answered D, you might be a motorhead. Or you might be an interested, concerned car owner who wants to better understand the new technology built into that shiny vehicle in the driveway. If you answered A, B, or C, this is the book for you! These pages will help de-mystify the modern automobile and identify its components and technology in simple, understandable terms.

Let's briefly decode the engine description:

DOHC—double overhead camshaft
EFI—electronic fuel injection
3.5L—3.5-liter displacement
L5—inline five-cylinder

But you knew all that, didn't you? If you're a hardcore motorhead, you did. You can, in fact, talk the talk and

walk the walk. But for the rest of us, let's take a closer look at the powerplant under the hood of your vehicle.

The basic concept of your car's engine is precisely what auto-motive describes—self-propelled. The engine is an air pump that provides the power to drive or move the vehicle. Simple enough, but how does it do this? By converting the energy contained in the fuel into heat, and converting that heat into power.

The first step is pretty simple: burn the fuel, release the BTUs of energy contained in the fuel. You could do this with a match, lighting the vapors from a small puddle of gasoline on the ground, but it wouldn't move your car very far, not to mention the possibility of it putting you in the hospital! So, the next step is to somehow harness that energy and turn it into work.

That's where the internal combustion engine comes into play. To understand the process, let's focus on a single-cylinder engine like one you might find on your lawnmower. The fuel is metered into the engine through the carburetor, where it is atomized (broken into tiny little droplets), then vaporized, mixed with air, and drawn through the intake manifold and intake valve into the cylinder. Now, the camshaft closes the intake valve as the piston starts up toward the top of the cylinder. The air/fuel mixture—ideally 14.7 parts air

THE FOUR STROKES OF A FOUR-CYCLE ENGINE

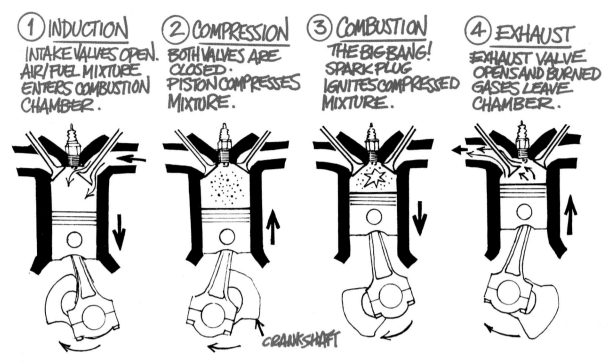

① INDUCTION INTAKE VALVES OPEN. AIR/FUEL MIXTURE ENTERS COMBUSTION CHAMBER.

② COMPRESSION BOTH VALVES ARE CLOSED. PISTON COMPRESSES MIXTURE.

③ COMBUSTION THE BIG BANG! SPARK PLUG IGNITES COMPRESSED MIXTURE.

④ EXHAUST EXHAUST VALVE OPENS AND BURNED GASES LEAVE CHAMBER.

CRANKSHAFT

to 1 part fuel—is compressed as the piston approaches the top of the cylinder, squeezing the mixture into the combustion chamber.

At precisely the right instant, a set of points operated off the distributor shaft open, collapsing a magnetic field in the ignition coil, creating a high voltage spark which jumps across the electrodes of the spark plug protruding into the combustion chamber. This action lights the fire and starts the combustion process. The air/fuel mixture burns progressively but extremely quickly, generating a tremendous amount of heat and pressure in the cylinder (but it doesn't explode). Substitute electronic fuel injection and electronic spark control for the carburetor and ignition points, and you've got the basics of a modern automobile engine.

How does the engine convert this burning process into work? The 1,600 degrees Fahrenheit of heat and tremendous pressure of rapidly expanding combustion gases apply massive pressure on the top surface of the piston, driving the piston downward in the cylinder. The piston is mechanically connected to the connecting rod, which transmits this force to an offset journal on the crankshaft—which applies the combustion pressure as a rotational force on the crankshaft.

Now, multiply this process by the number of cylinders in the engine and by the rotational speed of the

crankshaft, and presto, you've got useable power to drive the vehicle. Did you follow all that?

Modern gasoline engines are four-stroke, meaning four separate piston movements are necessary to fully complete one power cycle. The four strokes are:

Induction—intake valve opens as piston moves downward, drawing air/fuel mix into combustion chamber.

Compression—intake valve closes, piston moves upward in cylinder, compressing mixture.

Combustion—spark ignites mixture near top of piston stroke, generating heat/pressure that forces piston down cylinder.

Exhaust—exhaust valve opens as piston starts back up the cylinder, forcing burned gases out of combustion chamber.

Historically, two-stroke gasoline engines enjoyed the benefit of very light weight and high power-to-weight ratios. But inefficiency and higher emissions have moved two-strokes to the automotive sidelines. Just so you understand, here's how a two-stroke engine operates.

Rather than camshafts and valves that open and close to allow the air/fuel mixture into, and the exhaust gases out of, the engine, ports or openings in the cylinder wall are uncovered and covered by the movement of the piston. Since the piston can do this with each up/down movement, the engine can fire the air/fuel

FOUR TYPICAL ENGINE LAYOUTS

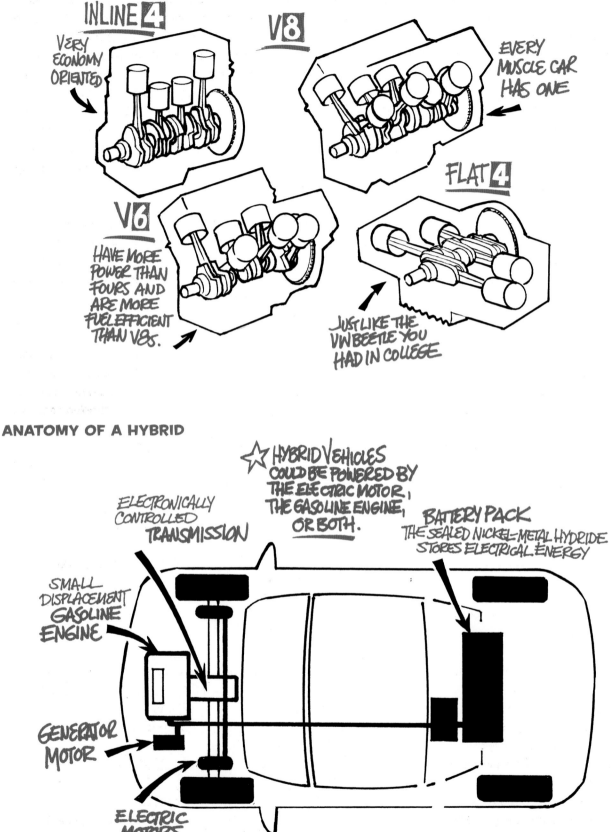

INLINE 4

VERY ECONOMY ORIENTED

V8

EVERY MUSCLE CAR HAS ONE

V6

HAVE MORE POWER THAN FOURS AND ARE MORE FUEL EFFICIENT THAN V8s.

FLAT 4

JUST LIKE THE VW BEETLE YOU HAD IN COLLEGE

ANATOMY OF A HYBRID

☆ HYBRID VEHICLES COULD BE POWERED BY THE ELECTRIC MOTOR, THE GASOLINE ENGINE, OR BOTH.

ELECTRONICALLY CONTROLLED **TRANSMISSION**

BATTERY PACK THE SEALED NICKEL-METAL HYDRIDE STORES ELECTRICAL ENERGY

SMALL DISPLACEMENT **GASOLINE ENGINE**

GENERATOR MOTOR

ELECTRIC MOTORS CAPTURE ENERGY THAT IS NORMALLY LOST DURING BRAKING

mixture each cycle rather than every other cycle as in the four-stroke engine.

As the piston moves downward on its power stroke, it uncovers the exhaust port to expel the hot exhaust gases and uncovers the intake port to draw in a fresh air/fuel charge. Since the engine's crankcase is effectively pressurized with the incoming air/fuel mix, uncovering these ports allows the exhaust gases to escape and pushes the incoming air/fuel mixture into the cylinder. As the piston continues upward, the charge is compressed and then ignited and burned at the top of the piston's stroke. Voila, the advantage of the two-stroke—power with every downward cycle of the piston.

DIESEL ENGINES

What about diesel engines? Diesels are gaining popularity for passenger-car use today for one simple reason: better fuel economy. The nature of diesel combustion is about 5–10 percent more efficient at converting the BTU energy in the fuel into actual work. Diesels can be two- or four-stroke, with the major difference being the nature of ignition. There are no ignition coils or spark plugs in diesels. The air/fuel mixture is heated and compressed to much higher levels as the piston moves toward the top of the cylinder, until it reaches its flash point and self-ignites. This time, there is an explosion, that's why you can hear the audible combustion process of a diesel.

HYBRIDS

In the past few years, a new type of engine has found its way under the hood—the hybrid. Hybrid means a mix, amalgam, or crossbreed of two different things. Literally hybrid engines mate two different power technologies into an integrated powerplant. Typically, hybrids incorporate a high-efficiency gasoline engine and some type of electric drive to boost performance and reduce dependence on the gasoline engine.

Honda's Insight, on the market for several years now, features a small 1-liter gas engine supplemented by an 8-horsepower electric motor mounted between the engine and manual transmission. The vehicle starts out on gas power, then adds the electric boost when needed. A sophisticated battery pack operates the electric motor and recharges while driving. Toyota's Prius is similar, but very different. The Prius utilizes an electric motor to get the vehicle underway, then brings the small gas engine online at roughly eight miles per hour. Recently, several carmakers have introduced sophisticated four-wheel-drive hybrid systems on light trucks and SUVs.

The obvious benefit of hybrid drives is efficiency—lower consumption of fossil fuels. More hybrid drive systems are currently in development and headed toward the market as consumer, industry, and government's focus on alternative fuels and power sources intensifies.

MODERN COMBUSTION TECHNOLOGY

Don't count the good old internal combustion engine out quite yet. With well over 100 years of development, modern gasoline and diesel engines are remarkable, refined, and efficient. Lots of new technology has been

HOW OVERHEAD CAMSHAFTS WORK

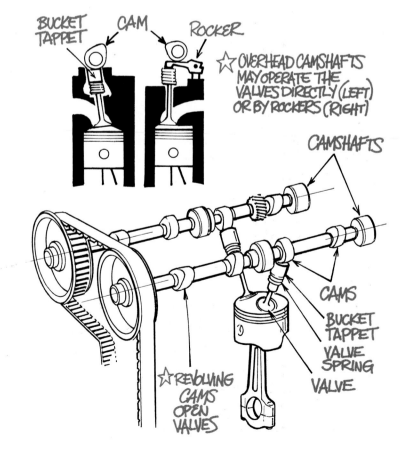

BUCKET TAPPET   CAM   ROCKER

☆ OVERHEAD CAMSHAFTS MAY OPERATE THE VALVES DIRECTLY (LEFT) OR BY ROCKERS (RIGHT)

CAMSHAFTS

CAMS

BUCKET TAPPET

VALVE SPRING

VALVE

☆ REVOLVING CAMS OPEN VALVES

applied to improve performance and efficiency and reduce emissions. None of it is new in the sense of just being discovered, but modern technology, design, engineering, and manufacturing have brought these into the automotive mainstream.

Overhead camshaft: by mounting the cam, or camshafts, on top of the cylinder head and operating the valves either directly or by rocker arms, fewer parts and lighter weight benefit the efficiency of the valvetrain.

Four valve: instead of a single intake and exhaust valve for each cylinder, a pair of intake valves and a pair of exhaust valves per cylinder allow better metering and control of incoming air and outgoing exhaust flow. In fact, even five-valves-per-cylinder engines—three intake and two exhaust—are commonplace these days.

Supercharging: by definition, supercharging describes forcing air into the engine under pressure rather than relying upon vacuum and atmospheric air pressure to fill the cylinders. By forcing more air into each cylinder, the effect is to make a little engine think it's a big engine and produce more power.

Supercharging describes a mechanically driven air pump that provides boost or high pressure air into the induction system. Belt or gear driven off the crankshaft, superchargers provide quick throttle response at relatively low rpm, making them well suited to bigger, lower-revving engines.

Turbocharging: when an exhaust-driven air pump is powered by the hot, rapidly expanding exhaust gases, the engine is being turbocharged. Turbos take a moment to spool-up to 20,000–30,000 rpm as the throttle is open, thus creating just a bit of throttle lag. But they work very well with small engines, helping them produce big power at higher rpm, yet still delivering the fuel mileage of a small engine.

Fuel injection: see Chapter 2 on Fuel Systems. The primary benefit of fuel injection is to inject the fuel under pressure to better atomize the fuel as it enters the induction system. This makes it vaporize into a burnable gas more efficiently. Earlier generations of mechanical fuel injection were efficient but mechanically complex and not well suited to daily passenger car operation. Mechanical injection systems have been the standard in big diesel engines in over-the-road trucks for decades.

Electronic fuel injection: this system has revolutionized fuel delivery. Computerized control of fuel delivery to each cylinder has revitalized the gasoline internal combustion engine with power and performance, efficiency and low emissions, along with incredible durability and reliability.

Electronic ignition: like EFI, electronic ignition systems have eliminated most mechanical/moving parts, increased accuracy and control of ignition timing, and improved performance, efficiency, drivability, and durability.

Distributor-less ignition systems (DIS): see Chapter 4. DIS eliminate the distributor entirely and provide multiple ignition coils, in some cases one coil per cylinder, mounted directly on top of the spark plug.

Variable valve timing: This provides electro-hydraulic control of valve timing (when the intake/exhaust valves open/close) by varying the timing relationship between the crankshaft, camshaft, and valves. It improves efficiency by allowing optimal valve timing at any rpm. Particularly useful in helping smaller engines deliver good power at low rpm.

Displacement on demand (DOD) or multiple displacement system (MDS): DODs or MDSs allow for disabling individual cylinders during specific operational parameters, i.e. cruise speed where less power is needed. This can be accomplished electronically be disabling spark and fuel to specific cylinders with the benefit of increased fuel mileage.

Whew, now you know why you recognize virtually nothing when you look under the hood of a modern automobile. In fact, carmakers have cleaned up the under-hood area with plastic shrouding that not only improves the visual appearance of the engine, but makes recognizing and servicing specific components even less of a DIY project. Thankfully, carmakers have identified and located the essentials—dipsticks for oil/transmission fluid, coolant recovery tank/cap, battery, etc.—so that car owners can find and check them, if they choose to do so.

You do choose to, don't you? Check the oil and coolant levels once a month, or more frequently if you know the engine consumes oil or anti-freeze. The two life-bloods of your engine are its oil and coolant. Said differently, running significantly low (or running out!) of either fluid is damaging at best, destructive at worst. So, once per month before you start the engine, pop the hood with your car parked on level ground in your garage, driveway, or the street. You do know where the hood release is, don't you? Remember, the information is in the owner's manual.

HOW TO CHECK YOUR COOLANT

With the engine completely cold, visually inspect the level of coolant in the coolant recovery tank—typically a translucent plastic reservoir in the engine compartment. It will be marked with a "cold" level mark and a "hot" level mark. If the level is significantly below the cold mark, top the reservoir up with a 50/50 mix of the correct anti-freeze and water. If the reservoir is empty (again, make sure the engine is fully cold) remove the pressure cap on the radiator and check the coolant level visually. If it's significantly low in the radiator, top up the reservoir and begin monitoring the levels weekly. If the level continues to drop, have a professional check the cooling system (see Chapter 3).

Or go directly to the shop and have a professional check the cooling system. Automobile's should not leak or consume measurable amounts of coolant. Fractional losses, perhaps a pint or less a year, are relatively normal. Any greater loss rate warrants testing.

HOW TO CHECK YOUR OIL

Next, pull the oil dipstick out, wipe it clean with a clean paper towel or cloth, reinsert it fully, pause for a moment, pull it out again, and check the level of oil. It should be within the hash marks on the dipstick, hopefully at or close to the "full" mark. If it's more than a half-quart low—below the middle of the hash marks—top the engine up with a half-quart of the correct viscosity oil. Remember, the engine's oil is the also the coolant for the mechanical and reciprocating components. Better "full" than "add" on the dipstick.

And change the oil and filter every 3,000–5,000 miles. Look at your owner's manual and read the description of "severe service" driving conditions. You qualify, right? The vast majority of car owners do. Granted, today's oils are far better products, and today's engines feature much better design, engineering, and metallurgy. Closer tolerances and tighter fits tend to reduce the rate of oil consumption and contamination. But remember this absolute reality: Regardless of warranty, regardless of service recommendation, *it is your vehicle and your engine*. Think of frequent oil/filter changes as cheap insurance against premature engine wear. Better safe than sorry.

And use premium quality oils and filters. Brand names tend to reflect a quality product—the company put its name and reputation right on the container or box. Nothing wrong with store brand oils/filters as long as they meet the correct American Petroleum Institute (API) service rating and Viscosity Index, but sticking with a reputable brand name oil and filter just makes sense. And doesn't cost much more, anyway.

OIL CHANGE COSTS

Speaking of costs, are you concerned that you're wasting money with frequent oil changes? Do the math. Calculate what two extra $25 oil changes per year add to your overall cost of owning, depreciating, operating, fueling, maintaining, repairing, licensing, insuring, and driving the vehicle. If you drive 15,000 miles per year, that extra $50 adds $0.0033 per mile to your costs. With the typical per-mile cost for newer vehicles in the $0.50 to $0.75 range, the extra oil changes are literally a drop in the bucket, a non-factor.

SYNTHETIC OILS

What about synthetic lubricants? Are they worth it? We could spend an entire chapter discussing the pros and cons of using synthetic oils, but the simple fact is that synthetic lubricants are fractionally better oils with the specific benefit of better initial flow on a cold start, better viscosity stability over the life of the oil, and better viscosity at higher operating temperatures.

Again, premium petroleum lubricants are wonderful products and perfectly suited for use in modern automobile engines, but if you want the last few percentage points of protection, by all means use synthetic lubricants. Again, the economics are not outrageous; the extra $10–$25 per oil change typically won't be a huge factor in the overall cost of the vehicle over the years you own and drive it. Besides, your engine will know how much you love it! And the oil change label on the windshield or doorpost indicating synthetic oil certainly won't hurt the resale value if you choose to sell the vehicle.

If you choose to use synthetic oil, can you dramatically increase the oil change intervals for your engine? No. Carmakers do not differentiate between synthetic and petroleum oils in their oil change recommendations, and neither should you.

How's that for a complete maintenance program? Just check and change the oil/filter and coolant periodically. If there's a transmission fluid dipstick, check this fluid every month or so as well, or at least at every oil change. That's if you *can* check the transmission fluid. . . . A number of newer vehicles have sealed transmissions with no dipstick.

AIR CLEANER CHANGES

Add a fresh air cleaner once per year and you've just about covered the necessary maintenance for the first 100,000 miles of driving. Compare that to the annual maintenance on vehicles of just a few decades ago and you'll see that carmakers have come to fully understand that most car owners *do not* care to spend the time, energy, or money to maintain their motor vehicles. So they are building much, much better vehicles that require far less maintenance!

Your motor vehicle will live with just this level of maintenance. But you're a conscientious car owner, right? You want to absolutely maximize how long your vehicle lasts, and minimize repairs over that period of time. Who doesn't? So, add a few more maintenance items before that first tune-up with fresh spark plugs at 100,000 miles.

Other Checks

Speaking of spark plugs, even if they're not scheduled for replacement until 100,000 miles, it's not a bad idea to remove, check, and reinstall them in the 30,000–50,000 range. If for no other reason, you can apply a small dab of anti-seize to the threads to prevent the plugs from rusting/sticking in the cylinder heat, particularly if the cylinder head is aluminum. Stuck plugs at 100,000 or more miles is not that uncommon (see Project 9, Change Plug Wires and Plugs).

Another item check is the positive crankcase ventilation (PCV) valve/filter. The PCV valve, if your engine is fitted with one, should be checked once per year to make sure it's clear and not clogged with oil/sludge. Usually mounted in the valve cover, just pull

THE TIMING BELT

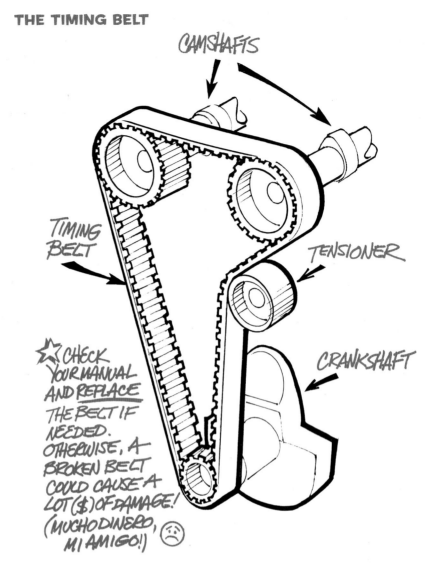

CAMSHAFTS

TIMING BELT

TENSIONER

CRANKSHAFT

☆ CHECK YOUR MANUAL AND REPLACE THE BELT IF NEEDED. OTHERWISE, A BROKEN BELT COULD CAUSE A LOT ($) OF DAMAGE! (MUCHO DINERO, MI AMIGO!) ☹

out the valve, shake it to make sure it rattles properly, look into the opening to check for sludge, and if it's still good, reinstall it. If it's plugged, buy and install a new one for just a few dollars. Ditto the PCV filter (if so fitted) in the air cleaner housing. And ditto if there's an exhaust gas recirculation (EGR) filter.

You also need to pay some attention to belts, hoses, the thermostat, and the radiator cap (see Chapter 5 for a more in-depth discussion of these). Visually inspect these items once per month when you have the hood open to check the oil and coolant. Four years or between 60,000–80,000 miles is a good yardstick for replacement of drive belts, hoses, thermostat, and radiator cap.

The timing belt drives the valvetrain of your car and is an internal belt that you cannot see when you open the hood of the car. (Not to be confused with the serpentine or V-style belt for the water pump and accessories, which is an exposed belt that you can see when you open the hood.)

Check your owner's manual to determine two specific things:

1. Does your engine utilize a rubber/fabric timing belt, or steel timing chain?

Timing belts often need periodic replacement in the 60,000–100,000-mile interval. Timing chains do not need periodic replacement.

2. Is your engine an interference engine? If so, if/when the timing belt or chain should fail or break, physical contact between open valves and pistons can occur, causing serious engine damage. If it's not an interference engine, then belt or chain failure will stop the vehicle in its tracks, but won't cause additional damage beyond the inconvenience and not insignificant cost of replacement.

The message here: follow the carmaker's recommendations for timing belt replacement. If you ignore the timing belt maintenance and it breaks, your engine could be ruined and cost you thousands of dollars in repairs.

DEALING WITH LEAKS

And finally, over many thousands of miles your engine may develop leaks of one type or another—oil, coolant, or fuel(!). How should you deal with a leak? First, know about it. If you don't open the hood once a month to check the oil and coolant and visually survey the engine compartment, how are you going to know there's a leak?

- The stain on the driveway/garage floor or office parking spot?
- The hot oil smell from under the hood?
- The waft of smoke from the engine compartment?
- The bittersweet aroma of hot anti-freeze?
  or
- Engine/transmission failure!

All of the above are red flags. Open the hood; look, smell, feel for evidence of leaks. Or put a piece of cardboard, newspaper, or a large sheet of white paper under your car overnight. If you find fresh stains on the sheet in the morning, something is leaking. The color of the stain can help you identify where the fluid is coming from, and the specific location under the vehicle can help pinpoint the source.

Brownish black oil—engine, transmission, transfer case, differential
Reddish, lighter color oil—transmission, power steering
Colorless, less oily—hydraulic brake fluid
Green or yellow, watery—anti-freeze/coolant
Watery, aromatic—gasoline!

Extremely minor oil leaks, such as dampness around or near a valve cover, are not particularly significant. You and your engine can live with this type of minor leak as long as you don't allow the oil level in the engine to drop below a safe level. But minor leaks have a way of becoming major leaks when left to their own devices. So, in some cases snugging or retightening valve cover bolts (for example) might slow or stop the leak, at least for awhile. But either way, until the leak leaves drops or puddles on the pavement, it may not be worth the several hundred dollar cost for a professional repair, particularly on an older, higher mileage vehicle.

But that doesn't mean you can't fix it yourself. Replacing valve cover gaskets is relatively straightforward; the only real issue is accessibility. If you can get to all the retaining bolts or nuts and the valve cover

LEAKS: THE PAIN OF GARAGE FLOOR STAINS

THE STAINS ARE THERE. DEAL WITH THEM! IDENTIFY THE SOURCE: ENGINE OIL? TRANSMISSION OR POWER STEERING FLUID? RADIATOR COOLANT, MAYBE? AND REMEMBER, CHANGING THE CARDBOARD WILL NOT SOLVE THE PROBLEM.

THE DREADED STAINS!

comes off cleanly without having to remove a variety of components or harnesses to give it clearance, it's a DIY project. Make sure you have the right tools—socket or wrench, extension, ratchet, etc.—and stop by the local auto parts store to pick up the replacement gasket and supplies, like gasket scraper or single edge razor blades, gasket sealer, and aerosol brake cleaner. Make sure it's the correct gasket. There's nothing more frustrating than getting everything apart, cleaned up and ready to reassemble . . . only to find you're holding the wrong gasket in your hand. Ask me how I know this.

With the engine cool and wearing a light pair of gloves, move or clear any stuff in the way, then unscrew (righty tighty, lefty loosy) the bolts or nuts that hold the valve cover in place. If the cover is stuck in place, a light tap with a rubber mallet should loosen it up. Pull it up and off the engine. Remove every single trace of old gasket material from the mating surfaces on both the valve cover and cylinder head—every trace! Use the gasket scraper or razor blade, then use something like Scotch-Brite™ to clean and polish the surfaces.

If the valve cover doesn't utilize a gasket, squeeze a uniform bead of sealer on the mating surface, then lay the valve cover in place. If it calls for a new gasket, squeeze a dab of sealer between your thumb and forefinger, then rub it onto both sides of the gasket to form a thin film. This also works well to help hold the gasket in place during assembly and seal it from leakage.

Stick the gasket to either the valve cover or cylinder head, lay the cover in place, reinstall and finger-tighten the fasteners, then snug them in place following a staggered pattern. There may be a specific fastening torque for these nuts or bolts; if you have a torque wrench, use it. If you don't, snug the fasteners firmly holding the ratchet in the palm of your hand. Hmm, the tool list was a bit longer than you first thought, wasn't it? That's why it's always a good idea to plan and review the job and gather every tool you could possibly need before starting the project.

Any significant or major oil leak or any type of coolant or fuel leak needs immediate attention. Particularly a fuel leak. If you ever smell raw gasoline or see raw gasoline in the engine compartment or on the pavement, you'd be well advised not to even start the engine. Remember, fuel injected engines deliver fuel under very high pressure, so any type of leak is an immediate and serious fire hazard. Just don't.

COOLANT LEAKS

You can identify a coolant leak by the color of the fluid coming out of the car. Coolant is generally green, yellow, or orange. Coolant leaks don't present quite the same level of risk as a fuel leak, but grossly overheated engines have been known to catch fire and burn. More so, any type of measurable coolant leak means there's a problem with the cooling system that could potentially lead to overheating and engine damage.

With the engine cooled down, you may be able to visually find the source of the coolant leak. It may be from a hose where it fits onto the radiator or engine outlet. Maybe it's just a loose hose clamp, if you're lucky. Or it may be dripping off the lower radiator hose—typical of a leaking water pump seal. Or the bottom of the radiator itself may be wet—potentially indicating a leak from the radiator itself. Or it may be dripping off the side or back of the engine—which can point to a corroded and leaking frost, or casting plug.

And in most cases, little leaks eventually become big leaks, so why wait until it's a major problem. Take the vehicle to a shop to find and fix the leak. In an emergency or for a short term fix for minor coolant leaks, you can try adding a stop-leak product to the radiator. To ease your mind about the usefulness of these products, many carmakers add a stop-leak product to the cooling system on their new vehicles to make sure there's no coolant dripping on the pavement when you park that new $30,000 machine in your driveway.

The bottom line on your engine is simply this: the engine is probably the strongest, most reliable and long lasting component on your vehicle. Most vehicles will expire due to corrosion or crash damage long before they suffer an engine failure, as long as the engine is maintained properly and not allowed to run low on oil or coolant, or overheated.

Said differently, the vast majority of engine failures are due to owner neglect and ignorance, not mechanical condition or wear. ▍

ENGINE TROUBLESHOOTING

PROBLEM	PROBABLE CAUSES	ACTION TO REPAIR
ENGINE LOCKED UP (won't turn over even with functioning battery and starter)	Hydraulic lock with fuel, water, or coolant	Remove spark plugs, pull fuses to disable ignition/fuel injection. Try starter/try to turn engine with socket on crankshaft pulley nut/bolt
	Mechanical failure—seized bearing/broken rod/piston/valve	Replace engine
EXCESSIVE BLUE SMOKE FROM TAILPIPE	Oil smoke from worn piston rings/valve guides/seals	Replace valve seals—may reduce oil smoke/consumption
	Plugged/blocked PCV valve	Replace PCV valve/check PCV hoses/fittings
ENGINE STOPS ENTIRELY	ECM/Ignition/Fuel delivery problem	See Electrical System Troubleshooting
EXCESSIVE WHITE SMOKE FROM TAIL PIPE	Coolant leaking into combustion chambers. Possible cylinder head gasket/intake manifold gasket failure	Pressure test cooling system. Chemically test for exhaust hydrocarbons in coolant. DIY—remove spark plugs right after shutting down engine; look for white vapor from spark plug holes
	Unburned fuel from stuck injector	Replace fuel injector
BLUE SMOKE FROM EXHAUST PIPE WHEN YOU FIRST START THE CAR, THEN EXHAUST EMISSIONS NORMAL	Worn valve guides/seals. Oil leaks into combustion chamber after engine is shut down	Replace valve seals—may reduce smoke
LOUD BANGING, CLANKING, KNOCKING, RATTLE FROM ENGINE	Mechanical noise from worn engine bearing/broken valve train component, worn/loose timing chain	Do not operate engine/drive vehicle until checked by a professional. DIY—use mechanical stethoscope to locate source of noise
	Loose bolt on torque converter hitting inside of bell housing	Retighten bolt—potential torque converter problem
ENGINE SPRAYS OIL OVER ENGINE COMPARTMENT	Loose oil fill cap	Tighten or replace cap
	Loose PCV valve	Re-insert PCV valve
	Oil leak from valve cover/cylinder head/main seal/oil pan	Identify and repair leak
LOW OIL PRESSURE LIGHT ILLUMINATES OR GAUGE SHOWS LOW OIL PRESSURE	Oil level low	Check oil and fill to manufacturer's recommended level. (Project 4: Check Oil and Project 5: Change Oil and Filter)
	Oil pump failing, worn engine bearings	Have engine/bearings/oil pump checked at professional service center
SMOKE FROM UNDER HOOD	Oil leak from engine dripping on hot exhaust	Identify and repair oil leak
	Hot coolant leaking from engine/radiator	Identify and repair coolant leak

Project 4
Check Oil

TALENT: 1

TIME: 5 minutes

TOOLS: Paper towel or rag

COST: $0

TIP: Check your oil at
          every fill-up or at least
          once a month. If the oil
          level is low, it will get
          dirty faster and accelerate
          engine wear.

4

CHECK OIL

1 Pull engine oil dipstick in engine bay.

2 Wipe the dipstick clean with a paper
towel or rag.

3 Reinsert the dipstick until the handle sits in its fully inserted position.

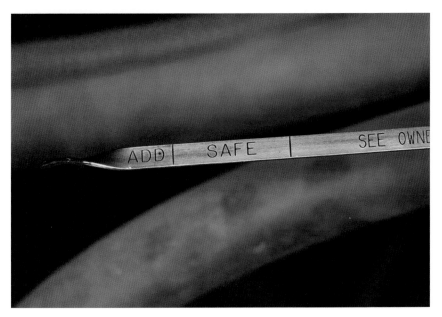

4 Pull the dipstick again and check the markings on the end for your engine oil's level. This engine's oil is fresh, so it is a translucent gold color. The streak of oil ends in the safe zone on the dipstick, indicating that the level is okay.

TIP: Check your oil once a month or about every 1,000 miles and maintain the recommended level, which will be indicated in your owner's manual. (Note that a given vehicle model's recommended level may vary by engine size.)

CHECK OIL

Project 5
Change Oil and Filter

TALENT: 2

TIME: 30 minutes

TOOLS: Funnel, drain pan, wrench, possibly an oil filter wrench

COST: $15–20

TIP: Stand the dirty filter threaded-side up in the filter box to prevent it leaking as you install the new one and add oil.

1 Changing your oil and oil filter regularly is essential to long engine life. Recommended intervals are included in your owner's manual. Oil is held in the oil pan on the bottom of the engine. The oil filter is located at left in this photo.

2 With the engine warm but not hot, remove the drain plug from the oil pan. Turn counterclockwise. Allow the oil to drain into a pan.

TIP: The plug is about 1/2-inch long. Don't let it drop into the drain pan.

3 Turn the oil filter counterclockwise to loosen. You might be able to free it by hand, but more likely you'll need an oil filter wrench, which any auto parts store and many convenience stores will carry. Some oil will drip when you loosen the filter so position your drain pan accordingly. Allow the oil to drain from the pan and filter area for a few minutes.

4 Wet the rubber seal on your new oil filter with fresh oil and thread it on. Snug the filter with the filter wrench, generally three-quarters to one full turn after the rubber gasket contacts the engine surface. Replace and fully tighten the oil drain plug.

Note: Be careful threading in the drain plug, as your pan will leak if you mess up the threads. Don't put the drain plug in with an air wrench; tighten it with a hand wrench.

5 The oil filler cap will be on top of the engine and labeled. Unscrew it and set aside.

CHANGE OIL AND FILTER

6 Insert a funnel in the oil filter hole.

7 Pour in the number of quarts prescribed in your owner's manual and replace the filler cap. Run your engine for a few minutes, then turn it off and check for leaks at the filter or filler plug. Recheck the oil level to make sure it's full.

Note: Make sure you properly recycle your old oil and filter. Many auto shops accept used oil and filters. Even many cities/counties will accept used motor oil and filters for recycling. Check with your local city offices.

Project 6
Change Air Filter

TALENT: 1

TIME: 5–15 minutes

TOOLS: None, screwdriver or small wrench, depending on style

COST: $10–$15

TIP: Check your air intake for obstructions such as leaves, particularly with the type that open to the grille.

1 Older air filters, as on this 1994 Dodge Dakota, typically reside in a round housing on top of the engine. Loosen the wing nut to open.

TIP: Check your owner's manual for service intervals (period of replacement) for your air cleaner and other maintenance items. If you use your vehicle in dirty settings, such as dirt roads or off-roading, check and replace the filter more often.

2 Lift off the metal lid.

3 Remove the filter element. This one is plenty dirty. Dirty filters reduce engine efficiency. Carefully wipe any dirt or debris from the air cleaner housing before replacing the filter element.

4 Newer vehicles typically have an air box, like this one, off to one side of the engine bay. You access the filter element by loosening a screw on a hose clamp or undoing a series of clips. The air filter then lifts out. Again, make sure the housing is clean before installing the new filter element. Note the orientation of the old filter and insert the new in the same direction.

Project 7
Change PCV Valve

TALENT:	2
TIME:	15 minutes
TOOLS:	None (hands)
COST:	$5–$15
TIP:	Remove the valve from the rubber grommet in the valve cover carefully to avoid damaging the grommet.

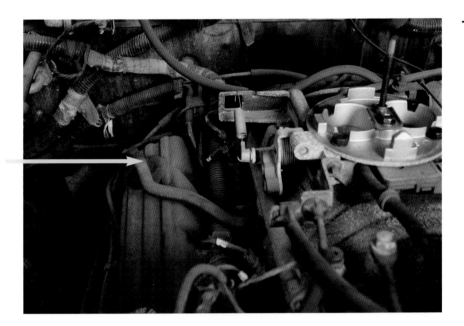

1 The PCV (positive crankcase ventilation) valve, if your engine is equipped with one, usually resides in the valve cover. Its job is to send combustion gases that escape into the valve cover up to the air intake, where they are drawn through the induction system and burned. Check your owner's manual for your PCV valve's service interval.

2 Pull the PCV valve out of the engine valve cover.

3 The valve may then be pulled from the hose running into the air cleaner.

4 Push the new valve into the hose.

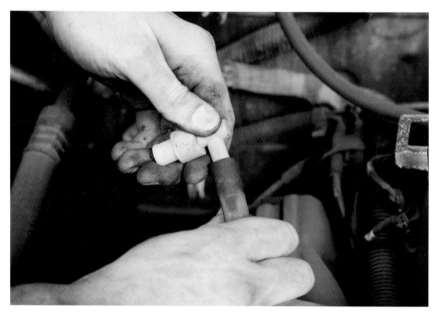

5 Press the other end of the valve into the rubber grommet in the valve cover. Make sure the valve is well sealed to the hose and valve cover.

Project 8
Replace Serpentine Belt

TALENT: 3

TIME: 15–45 minutes

TOOLS: Socket, long drive handle

COST: $20–$50

TIP: Observe the belt path carefully before you remove the old one and determine exactly how you want to thread the new one in to fit it properly.

1 A placard or sticker in the engine bay will explain how your serpentine belt is routed over and around the pulleys at the front of your engine. To change the belt, you need to find and release the belt tensioner to loosen the belt and create enough slack to remove it. This Dodge uses a pulley on a spring-loaded arm. The pulley is identified in the sticker, which also shows which way to move it for release. Some vehicles utilize a long threaded bolt to tighten the belt that must be unscrewed to relieve tension on the belt.

2 Place a socket on a long-handled ratchet or breaker bar over the nut on the tensioner pulley and push or pull in the direction indicated (here, inward).

3 With the belt loose, you can lift it off one of the pulleys and then thread it out, using the sticker for guidance. Do this task in broad daylight or with a bright shop light. If the placard or diagram is missing, draw the belt routing on paper before loosening and removing the belt. Better safe than sorry.

Tip: Remove the belt slowly and carefully. The easiest path for removing it is the easiest path for installing the new one.

Installing the belt is a bit like a puzzle. Study the routing sticker carefully to determine which pulleys to put it over and under. Give yourself time to get it right. When you find the proper route, you will need to crank the tensioner in again to give the new belt enough clearance to sit properly. Once installed and tight, double check the routing and make sure the belt is fully seated and properly positioned on each pulley.

Chapter 4
Electrical System

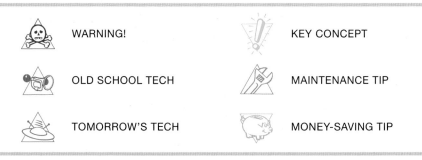

☠	WARNING!	⚠	KEY CONCEPT
📯	OLD SCHOOL TECH	🔧	MAINTENANCE TIP
🛸	TOMORROW'S TECH	🐷	MONEY-SAVING TIP

We think of our motor vehicles as gasoline or diesel powered, right? But stop for just a moment and think about how much of the vehicle is electrically powered. The list is amazing and growing yearly. From the starter motor to the lighting system; from the heating and air conditioning to the rear window defroster; from the power windows, seats, and door locks to the CD/stereo; from the windshield wipers to the ABS/traction control; from the instrumentation to the remote trunk/fuel door release; and of course, the entire electronic engine management/fuel injection system and electronically controlled transmission—without lots of those hard-working electrons, you're vehicle wouldn't move a foot.

Today's automotive electrical systems have reached a level of sophistication almost beyond imagination. All those electrically operated components and systems on today's motor vehicles require a lot of electricity and wiring to operate. And all that wiring, switching, connecting, processing, and operating has added up measurably to the complexity, sophistication, and costs of owning, operating, and servicing a modern motor vehicle.

THE BATTERY

Where to start? The origin of the electricity—the battery. Currently (pun fully intended), automotive batteries are rated at a nominal 12 volts. In actuality, the voltage at the posts of a fully charged battery should be 12.66 volts at room temperature, the sum of six individual cells each rated at 2.11 volts. This voltage is created chemically inside the battery when the liquid electrolyte—sulfuric acid and distilled water—washes over the lead plates in each cell. When new, fresh, and fully charged,

the battery can produce full voltage and maximum amperage—the current, or volume, of electricity the battery can deliver on demand. As the battery ages or is discharged, it's fully charged voltage can fall and its amperage output will drop until it won't start your vehicle.

WHY DO AUTOMOTIVE BATTERIES FAIL?

There are five primary reasons automotive batteries fail.

1 **Physical condition/deterioration**: Debris and sediment accumulate in the bottom of each cell, eventually bridging/shorting two cells together. Or an internal fracture or separation at a cell post physically breaks the circuit and kills the battery. A huge contributing factor in physical failure of a battery is improper, loose, broken, or failed battery mounting hardware. Loose batteries can, and do, fail prematurely from vibration and impact.

2 **Low electrolyte**: Is a maintenance-free battery really maintenance free? Not unless it's fully sealed, and even then it's not completely maintenance free. Maintenance free really means low-water-loss battery. The chemistry is complex but in simple terms. A lower percentage of antimony in the lead plate construction tends to reduce battery gassing as it's charged. This means less loss of electrolytes over the battery's life. Not no loss, just less loss.

3 **Corrosion**: You've seen it before, that nasty, white, pasty buildup on battery terminals and connections. This occurs from acidic electrolytes splashing or condensing on the terminals and rapidly corroding them to the point they can't:

   a) pass enough current to start/run the car; and/or
   b) won't accept recharging current from the alternator to keep the battery charged. Either way, the end result is the same, a dead battery.

BATTERY TERMINOLOGY

The basic terminology you need to understand in order to purchase, install, and maintain an automotive battery is relatively simple:

Size: typically listed as group size to describe the physical dimensions and characteristics of the battery. Your vehicle requires a specific group size battery for proper operation and installation. From 22-series to 98-series, the group size designation defines the voltage, number of cells, dimensional size, terminal style, location, and mounting/attaching style—all the critical information to determine the exact battery for your vehicle. There are also several universal batteries that fit many common vehicles and are priced very competitively.

Cold-cranking amps (CCA): the number of amperes (current) the battery can deliver continuously for 30 seconds at 0 degrees Fahrenheit while maintaining at least 1.2 volts per cell—7.2 volts for a 12 volt battery. Can you see how the CCA rating is the critical measure of the battery's ability to start your vehicle's engine in cold weather? The higher the CCA rating, the more amperage available to crank your engine, and the longer the battery will continue to crank it. If you live in a cold climate, it never hurts to purchase a replacement battery of the correct group size with a CCA rating 100–200 amperes higher than the carmaker's original specification. In cold weather, more CCA is definitely better. On small econo cars, reserve is more important than CCA.

Don't be confused by the cranking amps (CA) rating. This measurement is taken at 32 degrees Fahrenheit, which is useful for marine applications but doesn't give a true picture of the battery's ability to start your engine is freezing temperatures.

Reserve Capacity (RC)
Have you ever come back to your vehicle after an hour or so and found that you'd left the lights on? Or suddenly had the battery warning light illuminate on the dash while you're driving on the freeway? Did you initially panic that the you'd be stranded on the side of the road until the tow truck arrives to:

a) jump-start your engine;
b) replace your battery, alternator, or alternator belt; or, more likely
c) tow your dead vehicle to the garage for repair.

Well, if your vehicle's battery is still relatively fresh and fully charged, its reserve capacity may save the day. The reserve capacity rating defines how long the battery, at 80 degrees Fahrenheit, can deliver a continuous 25 amperes before its voltage drops below 1.75 volts per cell, or 10.5 volts for a 12-volt battery. Note that modern automotive batteries provide reserve capacities in the 60–120 minute range. This means that if/when the alternator or charging system fail, your vehicle's engine will continue to run for one to two hours, even on a cold night with the headlights, heater fan, and windshield wipers in operation, assuming the battery is relatively fresh and fully charged. Whether or not you choose to listen to the radio while hoping to make it home is your decision. Typically, the better quality the battery, the longer the reserve capacity relative to its CCA rating. Once again, more is better.

 When buying a new automotive battery, have you noticed how most warranties work? Free replacement for one, maybe two, and perhaps three years, then the battery is pro-rated for the remainder of the warranty—meaning its value is reduced by a progressive percentage until the warranty expires. Now, ask yourself this, "How long do the batteries in my vehicles usually last?" Three to six years, right? Does that explain why battery warranties are typically pro-rated after three years?

4   Sulfation: This *is* a dead battery. When an automotive battery is allowed to sit unused or in a discharged state for any significant period of time, the lead sulfate that builds up on the plates during the chemical reaction tends to harden into a solid mass that cannot chemically return to the electrolyte as the battery is recharged. That section of the plate is now dead for all time. This is why batteries tend to loose their CCA capability over time. Adding insult to injury, the electrolyte in a discharged battery is basically just water, which means it's quite capable of freezing in sub-32-degree-Fahrenheit weather. Once frozen, there's little hope of restoring a battery for operation.

5   Overcharging: This is the most subtle of battery failures. If the vehicle's charging system fails in such a way as to supply too high of a charging voltage to the battery, the battery electrolyte tends to boil away, leaving a much higher concentration of acid in the battery and shortening its life considerably. In many cases, there's no symptom or indication of this problem until the battery fails. The battery light in the dash probably won't illuminate, although the "check engine" light may come on from too high a system voltage. If your vehicle is equipped with an actual voltage gauge on the dash, you would see voltages above 15–16 volts continuously.

And here you thought that the one component in your vehicle that is pretty much a no-brainer was the battery. Well, it is . . . if you don't mind buying a new battery every couple of years.

If your vehicle absolutely, positively must start each and every time you need it, you would not be wrong to install a new battery every three years, or at the end of the battery's free-replacement warranty period. Wasteful? If you're a fireman, paramedic, plow truck driver, police officer—someone who absolutely, positively must get to work on time every day—consider this a relatively inexpensive insurance policy. For 25 bucks a year (a $75 battery divided by its three-year life) your vehicle, with an always-fresh battery, will always start when you need it to.

Perhaps in this case, no-brainer applies to the motorist rather than the battery.

BATTERY MAINTENANCE

The automotive battery under the hood of your car or truck should live six or more years with good maintenance and a little luck. There are no guarantees beyond the battery's warranty, of course, but a conscientious car owner willing to check, service, and clean the battery and its connections and terminals perhaps twice a year *should* (there's that word again) be able to have that battery start and run the vehicle for more than half a decade.

Taking care of your battery isn't particularly difficult, but there is some danger. Remember, batteries are filled with an electrolyte that contains sulfuric acid—not something you ever want to come into physical contact with. So, step number one in battery maintenance is the simple safety precaution of wearing gloves and eye protection *every time* you're working with the battery.

Is your battery ready to start your vehicle? Easy enough to check, just grab your handy-dandy digital voltmeter (which you can buy at Radio Shack or auto parts stores) and check the voltage across the terminals. As described above, a fully charged battery should be in the 12.6 volt range at room temperature. Accuracy is important here—which is why an inexpensive digital voltmeter is the best choice. A voltage reading of below 12.2 means the battery is only 60 percent charged and probably won't start your engine on a cold morning.

Check, clean, and retighten battery cables and connections twice a year. Wipe or brush off any dirt, grease, or corrosion from around the terminals, making sure the nasty white crud doesn't end up on something that will rust. And here's a great tip: pour a small amount of sugar-free diet soft drink on each terminal. The carbonation and acidity of diet pop does a pretty good job of washing away the build up of corrosion.

Physically check the tightness/security of the battery connections with your gloved hand. If at all loose, remove, clean, and reconnect securely. You might want to add a battery corrosion preventive to each terminal to prevent/slow any future corrosion. This product comes in several forms, including a spray paint, manually applied grease, and impregnated felt O-rings that fit under the clamps on a top-terminal battery. Even a light coating of petroleum jelly works well to reduce corrosion on battery terminals.

The connections on side terminal batteries are a bit more difficult to check. The advantage of protected, and somewhat physically sealed, connections can mask poor internal connections from cable to battery. Wiggle each cable connection firmly to check for any looseness or play whatsoever. If you find any, disconnect, clean, apply a bit of petroleum jelly, and reattach firmly.

If the battery has removable cell covers—either the individual screw-on covers or the pair of flat, square, rectangular, removable covers—pry them up and off gently and visually inspect the level of electrolyte in each cell. Gloves and eye protection are absolutely mandatory for this, as you're exposing the electrolyte/sulfuric acid. The battery should be fully charged when you make this inspection, otherwise the electrolyte level can be low due to the state of discharge. Filling the cells while the battery is significantly discharged can force excess electrolyte out of the vents as the battery is recharged.

If the top of the plates are exposed in any of the cells, add distilled water with a small squeeze-bulb turkey-baster tool. Use distilled water to reduce the mineral content and debris in the electrolyte, and add just enough to cover the top of the plates. Replace the cell covers, and don't forget to wipe the battery clean to remove any acid that may have splashed or accumulated on the top of the battery. Use paper towels and throw them directly into the trash when finished.

If you're hardcore, you can check the electrolyte in each cell with an inexpensive battery hydrometer. This turkey-baster-like syringe will allow you to draw a sample of electrolyte from each cell and determine its specific gravity, which is the measure of its state of charge. A reading of 1.265 indicates a fully charged cell, 1.120 means a fully discharged, dead cell. Look for any cell that's more than 0.5 below the average of the other cells.

But why bother with all the mess and risk? Just use your digital voltmeter to check the battery condition as described above.

THE BASIC ELECTRICAL SYSTEM

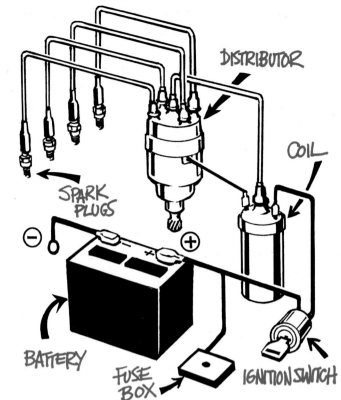

DISTRIBUTOR

COIL

SPARK PLUGS

BATTERY

FUSE BOX

IGNITION SWITCH

Finally—and this is the most overlooked aspect of battery maintenance—check the battery mounts, brackets, and fasteners carefully. Again, the battery needs to be solidly attached to the vehicle to minimize vibration, bouncing, and physical abuse. And here's another hint. Over time, the small amount of battery acid that escapes in the form of gas tends to start corroding the brackets and fasteners holding the battery in place. It's a good idea to flush them as clean as possible to remove any existing corrosion, then wipe or spray all the hardware with an aerosol grease or rust preventative. Even wiping a bit of petroleum jelly on these parts will help slow the inevitable rusting process.

The second important aspect of battery maintenance is to make sure the alternator, voltage regulator, and charging system are in good working order. Proper function of the charging system does just that; it keeps the battery topped up and ready to deliver full amperage the next time you turn the key to start the engine.

Maintenance Tip: You may have to reset your radio presets and time and any other electronic settings on your car (clock time, air bag deactivation, etc.) when you disconnect your battery.

Alternator and Charging System

So, how does that battery under the hood stay charged? Heck, the vehicle requires roughly 25 amperes of current to operate at night. That rate of current draw would run the battery flat within an hour or two unless there is some way to recharge the battery with the engine running. And there is: the alternator.

When carmakers first began installing starter motors and electrical systems on automobiles, they installed belt-driven generators to re-supply the battery with voltage. Generators are simply electric motors being mechanically driven to generate current rather than being electrically powered to motor, or drive, something. A mechanical voltage regulator kept the charging voltage relative constant over the working range of engine rpm, and if everything was working correctly, the battery stayed nicely charged.

Alternators replaced generators during the 1950s and 1960s. Alternators are smaller, lighter, and more efficient. But unlike generators, they produce alternating current (AC) rather than direct current (DC), which is what powers the vehicle's electrical system. No problem. Diodes and rectifiers rectified the AC current, allowing only DC current from the unit, and the voltage regulator turned the field current on and off fast enough to keep the charging voltage in the proper 13–15 volt range for a 12-volt system. In order to actually recharge or chemically reverse the discharge process in the battery, the charging system must produce voltage about 2 volts higher than the battery's roughly 12.5 volts. This higher voltage forces amperage back into the battery, so to speak, reversing the chemical reaction and recharging the battery.

The voltage regulator, whether the electrical device stands alone in the engine compartment or, more commonly, is built into the alternator itself or, more recently, is incorporated into the powertrain control module (PCM)—the engine management computer itself—does exactly what its name describes. By turning on and off the field current to the rotating field/armature in the alternator, it regulates output voltage in that 13–15-volt range and controls the recharging voltage to the battery. A voltage regulator failure can either allow the battery to progressively discharge as the vehicle is operated, or actually overcharge and kill the battery by supplying an overly high, unregulated voltage due to a component failure in the regulator.

THE ELECTRICAL SYSTEM (IN YOUR CAR)

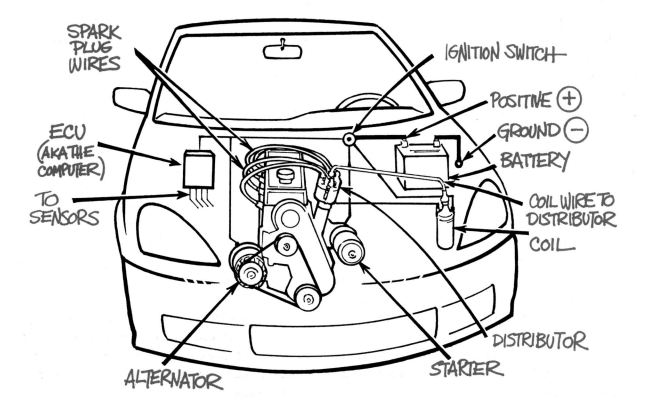

SPARK PLUG WIRES

IGNITION SWITCH

POSITIVE (+)

GROUND (−)

BATTERY

ECU (AKA THE COMPUTER)

TO SENSORS

COIL WIRE TO DISTRIBUTOR

COIL

DISTRIBUTOR

ALTERNATOR

STARTER

BATTERY CUTAWAY

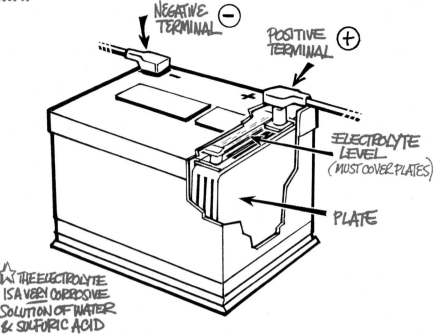

NEGATIVE TERMINAL ⊖

POSITIVE TERMINAL ⊕

ELECTROLYTE LEVEL (MUST COVER PLATES)

PLATE

☆ THE ELECTROLYTE IS A VERY CORROSIVE SOLUTION OF WATER & SULFURIC ACID

Thus modern automobiles feature a highly efficient, lightweight, compact alternator to provide the electrical current required to operate the vehicle. The alternator is driven by a belt on the front of the engine and requires little or no maintenance . . . until it fails. Just check the condition and tension of the drive belt, whether a conventional V-belt or multi-ribbed serpentine belt at each oil change, and keep the battery and alternator connections clean and corrosion free. The alternator is much closer to being maintenance free than the battery ever will be.

So, how do you know if the alternator on your vehicle is working properly? The gauge on the dashboard helps. Today's vehicles have either a battery warning light or a battery gauge. Earlier generations of cars and trucks had actual ammeters on the dash. An ammeter was a gauge which showed how much amperage was flowing to or from the battery. If the current flow was positive, the battery was recharging. If it was negative, the battery was discharging. This was, and still is, a faster indication of charging system performance. However, ammeters needed to carry current, which made the wiring and connections a bit more complex and heavy duty. Voltmeters are now the gauge-of-choice for displaying battery information on the dash. If the car does not have an ammeter or voltmeter, it is likely equipped with a simple red "batt" or "volt" warning light.

This warning light will come on when you first turn the key to the "on" position, then will go off shortly after the engine starts if the alternator is charging and everything is working properly. If this warning light illuminates solidly and continuously while driving, take the hint! Something's wrong with the battery and/or charging system. Specifically, this light will come on when system voltage produced and maintained by the alternator drops to within about 1/2 volt of the battery's nominal 12.5 volts. When this occurs, the alternator is not producing high enough voltage to recharge the battery and the battery will ultimately discharged as it provides current to run the car. See the Reserve Capacity section to get an idea of how long your vehicle will run before stalling and leaving you stranded on the side of the road. If you're smart, you'll make absolutely sure that your favorite automotive shop is well within that range.

It's important to note that there may be times in normal driving situations when the battery warning light will illuminate momentarily. You may, for example, see this light glow for a moment or two while waiting at a stop light in drive with the headlights, heater fan, and rear window defroster turned on. In this situation, the amount of current necessary to run the vehicle and all these accessories at low engine rpm may exceed the alternator's output momentarily. As long as the light goes out as soon as you drive away and engine rpm increases, there's probably no problem—probably.

However, if this hasn't happened before and starts happening more regularly, you'd be a wise motorist to check the battery and charging system.

If your vehicle is equipped with a battery gauge on the dash, familiarize yourself with its pattern of operation. When you first turn the key prior to starting the engine, this gauge should read a battery voltage of roughly 12.5 volts. Once the engine starts and the charging system comes on line, the voltage should rise into the 13–15 range.

If the charging system fails, you'll see this gauge progressively drop from the 14-volt range down toward 12 volts or even lower. Modern engines will stop running when voltage drops much below 11 volts, so if you see voltage dropping toward that nominal 12 volts, recognize that there's a problem before the car stalls.

Easy Test for Your Charging System

Is there a quick DIY charging system test? You bet. Grab that little handy-dandy digital voltmeter and check the battery voltage before starting the engine, as described earlier. Then get the engine started if you can—by replacement battery, recharged battery, or jump start—and recheck voltage at the battery. Your meter should read between about 13.5 and 15 volts, indicating that the charging system is trying to recharge the battery. If it stays in that 12-volt range and does not move as the engine starts, well, you better head for the parts store while it's still running because the alternator isn't recharging the battery.

STARTING SYSTEM

The starting system in your vehicle is perhaps the simplest electrical system, but the most important, of course. It consists of switches, wiring, and connections that operate a powerful starter motor that engages and spins the engine at 200–300 rpm to get it started.

When the key is turned to the spring-loaded "start" position, the ignition switch sends an electrical signal to the starter relay, and/or solenoid, which electrically switches on the starter motor and mechanically engages the starter drive gear. The starter relay, or solenoid, is basically a large electromagnetic switch that connects the battery to the starter motor. If the battery is strong, if the connections are clean and solid, if the engine is in tune, if the phases of the moon are aligned, then hopefully your engine will start right up.

Dealing with a No-Start Engine

We've all had that stomach-churning, heart-stopping staccato "click, click, click" from the starter relay/solenoid. Dead battery? Bad connection? Dead starter motor? Bad solenoid? The problem could be any or all of the above.

Check battery connections first. With your gloved hand (remember your safety glasses too), give each terminal/connection a firm wiggle test. If it moves, it's loose. Clean, retighten, and recharge the battery. Remember, more than 75 percent of no-starts are battery/connection related. If the battery and connections are good, the problem could be anywhere from the ignition switch to the starter relay/solenoid to the starter motor itself.

But before you start buying expensive replacement parts, remember this mantra: connections and grounds, connections and grounds, connections and grounds. In the majority of no-start situations, the problems are in connections or grounds.

The simplest DIY test? Take that same little digital voltmeter and measure battery voltage to chassis ground. In other words, touch the red/positive test lead to the "POS+" battery terminal, and the black/negative lead to any solid metal component on the engine or chassis. Obviously, you should read 12.6 volts if the battery's fully charged and capable of cranking your engine. Start at the battery itself, then work your way through every major positive connection leading toward the starter motor, with your gloves and eye-protection on, of course. If battery voltage is above 12.2–12.4, the engine should at least crank over a little bit. Maybe it won't start, but it'll give an indication of a willingness to crank, if enough amperage is available.

With a helper turning the key to start as you test, check voltage at each connection down the line. You're looking for no more than a 1/10-volt drop per connection. Anything more indicates a poor-quality, high-resistance connection that may well be the source of the no-start. If you find one, disconnect the battery to protect yourself and the vehicle, then disconnect, clean thoroughly with Scotch-Brite ®, or steel wool, and reassemble securely.

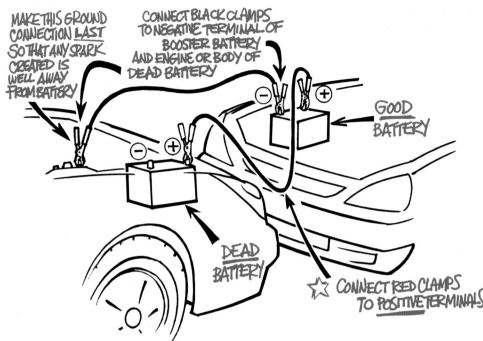

MAKE THIS GROUND CONNECTION **LAST** SO THAT ANY SPARK CREATED IS WELL AWAY FROM BATTERY

CONNECT BLACK CLAMPS TO NEGATIVE TERMINAL OF BOOSTER BATTERY AND ENGINE OR BODY OF DEAD BATTERY

GOOD BATTERY

DEAD BATTERY

☆ CONNECT RED CLAMPS TO POSITIVE TERMINALS

Quick Starting System Test

Is there a shortcut to troubleshooting the starting system? Yes, but you need to take great care in doing this. Since so, so many starting issues are due to poor connections and grounds, why not skip all that and apply battery voltage directly to the positive terminal on the starter motor? This should crank the engine, shouldn't it?

Yes, and it will, so take care. Here's the procedure. Put the transmission in park and leave the key turned to off; you don't want the engine to actually start, you just want to know if it will crank properly at this stage. Use your booster cables. (You do have a quality, heavy-duty set of booster cables in your emergency kit in the trunk, don't you?) Connect one end of the red/positive cable to the positive terminal on the battery, then with all your bodily parts and clothing clear of the fan and/or moving parts and wearing your eye protection, gloves, and full body armor, quickly touch the other end of the red/positive cable to the positive terminal on the starter motor. Make sure it's the positive terminal, of course, by tracing/following its cable back and confirming it goes through the solenoid, or relay, to the battery.

This momentary contact between the red cable from the positive terminal on the battery will likely produce a quick spark, but it should also begin to crank the engine at relatively normal cranking speed. If it does, the battery and starter are likely okay. If it does not and the starter just groans or clicks, you've found the problem—it's either the starter motor,

battery, or ground connection from the starter back to the negative post on the battery. So, one more test.

Keeping the red clamp away from the starter for the moment, connect the black/negative booster cable clamps to the battery's negative terminal and a solid bracket or component on the engine itself; the alternator mounting bracket often makes a convenient place for this ground. Now, quickly touch the red clamp to the starter's positive terminal again. Does it crank this time? If so, the problem is a bad chassis ground between the engine/drivetrain, body/frame, and/or negative terminal of the battery. Leave the battery disconnected and disassemble, clean, and re-secure all the major ground connections between these components.

Using Booster Cables

If the starter still doesn't crank the engine, you've narrowed it down to the starter or battery. Try safely jump-starting the vehicle with your booster cables. Wear your safety glasses and gloves, and remember the connection sequence. It's very, very important for your safety.

- Both vehicles switched off
- Red/positive clamp on positive terminal of helper battery
- Red/positive clamp on positive terminal of dead battery
- Black/negative clamp on negative terminal of helper battery

- Black/negative clamp on chassis ground well away from dead battery
- Start/fast idle helper car for 30 seconds, then start dead car
- Disconnect in reverse order

The key to safely using booster cables is to make that last connection—the connection that is most likely to create a spark—well away from the dead battery. Again, the alternator mounting bracket or even a strut tower mounting bolt will work. Why will a chassis ground work as well as the negative terminal on the battery? Because electrically they are the same. The negative terminal of an automotive battery is directly connected to the vehicle's chassis and drivetrain, so as long as the connections are clean and solid, the electrons trying to return to the battery don't care.

Remember what we learned earlier about the sulfuric acid and hydrogen sulfide gas produced by batteries? Well, guess what? It's explosive! A spark created in proximity to the battery or battery vents can—and has many times, much to the detriment of uninformed car owners—ignite/explode those gases and the battery itself. This is a real no-no, so don't forget this.

If/when the dead vehicle starts and you're sure it's going to stay running, remove the booster cables in the reverse order, starting with that final ground connection on the chassis of the dead car.

HOW DO YOU KNOW IF THE PART IS BAD?

Okay, you've done a great job of identifying that the no-start condition is either the battery or starter motor. Should you run off to the parts store and buy a new . . . battery? Or starter motor? Yes and no. Run off to the auto parts store, but take the battery and starter motor assembly with you. Many parts stores will test these components for you at no cost so that you'll know which component actually needs replacing. Nice of them, isn't it? But it's worth it to them because they sell batteries and starter motors. Quality starter/solenoid assemblies that feature good warranties are available as remanufactured units for significantly less than half the cost of brand new units.

By the way, auto parts stores can usually test alternators, voltage regulators, and ignition modules as well, so keep this in mind

before you try the dartboard approach to problem solving by purchasing a bunch of new parts. Remember, most automotive electrical parts and components are not returnable.

In fact, if you can get your vehicle running with a jump start, head straight to the auto parts store, leave it running, and ask them to test the alternator and charging system right on the vehicle.

LET THERE BE SPARK

A strong battery and solid starter motor can spin the engine over all day (well, not all day but plenty long enough) to start, if the ignition system is supplying and distributing the proper spark to each cylinder at precisely the right time. Unless you're driving a diesel, the gasoline vapors so carefully mixed and distributed to each cylinder can't burn properly to produce power unless they're ignited by a strong spark from the spark plugs. That's the job of the ignition system.

The earliest internal combustion gasoline engines utilized magnetos to produce spark. A magneto is a small generator built into a distributor. As the distributor shaft is rotated by the engine itself, the magneto's small coil produces an electrical spark that the distributor directs to the correct spark plug. Presto, ignition.

The magneto's primary limitation is the size of its coil and thus the intensity of its spark. So it wasn't long before carmakers introduced battery ignition systems on their engines. The simplest battery ignitions featured a battery to supply the basic current, an electrical coil to produce a very high voltage spark, a distributor to route the spark to the individual spark plug wires, and spark plugs to deliver that spark into the combustion chamber to ignite the air/fuel mixture.

The Heart of the Electrical System

The ignition coil is an elegantly simple device. Battery voltage is supplied to a tightly wound coil of wire that surrounds an iron core. This magnetizes the core. When the current is stopped suddenly, the magnetic field around the core collapses and a surge of electrical energy is directed through the plug wire to the spark plug. This electrical energy jumps across an air gap between two electrodes at the tip of the spark plug to produce a bright blue arc, or spark, which lights the fire in the combustion chamber.

For the engine to actually run, the coil must do this job hundreds of times a second! Thus, a trigger device of some kind is necessary to turn the current on and off to the coil.

Although some of the earliest engines featured a coil for each cylinder, making them early distributor-less ignition systems, most gasoline engines utilized a distributor to do two different jobs. First, the points in the distributor, operated by a small cam or lobe on the distributor shaft, closed to allow battery voltage to charge the coil. They then opened at the proper time to collapse the coil's magnetic field and produce a spark. The electrical condenser connected to the points helped to buffer the voltage and spark created by the points opening and closing, thus prolonging their life.

Can you see why a tune-up was so essential for so many years? Either a fresh set of points/condenser, or at least an adjustment of the air gap on the points to ensure the correct rise time—the amount of time current flowed into the coil to build the magnetic field—for the coil, helped ensure the engine ran smoothly, cleanly, and efficiently.

The second role of the distributor was to distribute the spark to each cylinder. The spinning shaft in the distributor was driven by the camshaft and rotated the rotor, which was electrically connected via a small air gap to the wire from the coil carrying the high voltage spark energy to the spark plug wire for each cylinder in the proper sequence. Loosening a pinch-bolt and rotating the body of the distributor allowed a range of adjustment to ensure proper timing of the spark delivery.

In essence, the distributor acted as the trigger to generate the spark from the coil, and then distributed that spark to the correct cylinder at the correct time. A mechanical marvel, for sure. Replacing and/or adjusting the points and then resetting the ignition timing were essential tune-up services that were needed at least once per year.

Electronic Control Modules

In the 1970s carmakers replaced the points inside the distributor with electronic components such as magnetic pick-up coils, (you'll love this one) Hall-effect transmitters, and electronic ignition modules. On many of today's engines, distributors have been eliminated entirely,

although there are still a number of engines with distributors being built. Ignition timing and control is now done by computer (are you surprised?). Sensors on the crankshaft and camshaft determine the rotational position of the crankshaft and pistons and feed this info to the engine management computer, which is programmed to trigger spark to each cylinder at a specific time. These systems still use coils to generate the spark, but utilize multiple coils. In some cases, there's an ignition coil for each cylinder, often mounted right on top of the spark plug.

Notice the first major advantage of this system over a distributor: no moving parts. No points, no distributor, no rotor, nothing to mechanically wear out, burn away, or break. And secondly, because of the microprocessor control of the ignition, electronic ignition systems deliver much more precise and accurate spark timing for each cylinder under all operating conditions. Today's ignition systems not only perform light-years better than their predecessors, but are far more durable and reliable, and require much less maintenance.

Accurate spark timing and fuel control mean spark plugs live much longer, and 100,000 miles between replacements is not uncommon today. Even spark plug wires last longer because of their high-quality materials and construction. But these secondary ignition components, carrying the extremely high voltage spark, are not life-of-the-vehicle parts and need to be check periodically.

Even engines that still utilize a distributor no longer have parts inside that need replacement. Instead of ignition points and condensers, modern distributors are fitted with electrical or electronic triggers—magnetic pick-up coils or Hall-effect transmitters. Although they have complex names, they are really simple devices that recognize and identify the specific rotational position of the engine in order to provide spark timing information to the ignition module—the little microprocessor that decides exactly when to supply a spark to each cylinder.

WHAT TO DO WHEN THINGS SHORT, FIZZLE, AND DIE

When the power windows stop working, the heater fan stops blowing, the turn signals stop flashing, or the horn won't beep, what you are you going to do? Take the car to the dealer? To an independent shop? To the corner gas station? (Are there corner gas stations anymore?) Or ask your motorhead neighbor to take a shot at the problem?

All of the above may be viable answers, but the one thing they have in common is that they do not include you in the problem-solving stage. You're only participation is to pull out your wallet and hand over a pile of money, or a six-pack if it's your gearhead neighbor.

But you're not completely helpless when it comes to troubleshooting electrical problems with your modern automobile. Yes, in many—perhaps even most—cases, you'll need professional help. But it's always worth trying the KISS principal first. The automotive application of this well-know concept is "check the simple stuff first."

Remember the basic nature of your vehicle's electrical system. It operates on 12 volts DC. Whether it's the electric fuel pump that supplies fuel to the engine, the electric motor that runs the window up and down, the fan that blows heat into the cabin, or the CD/stereo that thumps heavy metal through the speakers, all require a complete circuit for the electrons to travel. Current must flow from the positive battery terminal to the device, then from the device back to the negative battery terminal. In most cases, the devices are switched on and off by interrupting the power or ground connection.

The Fuses, Relays, and Connections (FRC) Principle

That means if an electrical component or system isn't working, check for simple causes first. FRC is not the rude utterance of frustration, it's "fuses, relays and connections." Just like a no-crank scenario due to battery connection or connection issues, most electrical problems can be traced to one of these three culprits:

A fuse is a simple protection device that limits the amount of electrical current a circuit can carry. In simple terms, the little wire in the fuse will burn up and fail if too much amperage tries to flow. Literally, your $30,000 motor vehicle is protected from fire and destruction by a number of 50-cent fuses. Of course, once a fuse fails, it must be replaced with a fuse of the exact same amperage rating. No fudging here, no installing higher amperage fuses to try to solve the problem.

A relay is simply an electrically operated switch. Sounds more complex than it is. A small current magnetizes a small coil, which pulls a set of contact points together, switching on that circuit. The advantage here is that only a small amount of current is need

to activate the switch that may carry lots of current to the heater fan, headlight, 600-watt stereo, etc.

A connection is just what the name suggests, the joining of two wires or circuits. Often, the connection is secured by a bolt or nut or involves some type of plug.

Familiarize yourself with the location and contents of the fuse and relay panels in your vehicle. Notice that it's plural, you may well find a fuse panel under or near the dash inside the car, and another fuse/relay panel under the hood. Many newer cars also feature fuse centers in the trunk and/or under the rear seat. So, identify where the fuses and relays are located in your vehicle.

Where will you find this information? In the owner's manual, of course.

Speaking of which, did you find the $10 bill that's inserted into the owner's manual of every new vehicle? Didn't know that carmaker's did this, did you? Well, the fact that you didn't know this means you haven't read your owner's manual. If you had, you'd have discovered they don't. I'm actually sharing an old trick used by fleet managers for years—this was the only way they could trick their drivers into spend a few moments familiarizing themselves with the specific vehicle they were driving.

So no, carmaker's don't put money between the pages of the owner's manuals, but they do fill those pages with useful information—like the identity, rating, and function of each fuse, and simple troubleshooting information to help you deal with roadside problems.

In fact, the only electrical systems/circuits that are not protected by replaceable fuses are the headlights/running lights, which are usually operated by a relay and protected by an internal circuit breaker in the headlight switch, as well as momentary contact circuits like power windows/door locks, power seats, and remote trunk/hatch releases. Often, these components will also be powered by relays and protected by thermal circuit breakers. ▦

ELECTRICAL SYSTEM TROUBLESHOOTING

PROBLEM	PROBABLE CAUSES	ACTION TO REPAIR
ENGINE WON'T CRANK	Dead battery	Clean and tighten battery connections, look for loose wires. *(Project 14: Clean Battery Posts)*
	Poor electrical connections	Recharge/replace battery. *(Project 16: Replace Battery)*
	Worn ignition switch	Check and replace ignition switch
	Bad starter relay switch	Replace starter relay switch
		Check for voltage at small terminal on starter/solenoid with ignition turned to "start." If no voltage, check ignition switch and park/neutral safety switch
	Faulty/misadjusted park/neutral safety switch	Jump/bridge connections on switch for test. If engine cranks, switch is "open" or transmission is not in park or neutral
	Mechanical problem of hydraulic lock	See Engine Troubleshooting chart
ENGINE CRANKS BUT WON'T START	Car is out of gas	Check fuel level
	Fuel pump relay or fuse is bad	Check fuel pump relay and fuse. *(Project 17: Test and Replace Fuses)*
	Fuel pump failed	Check fuel pressure at fuel rail test port. After turning key on/off 6 times, with key off hold rag about 6 inches above test fitting, and depress small "pintle". You should see one strong squirt of fuel from fitting. If there is no squirt or there is just a dribble of fuel, there is no fuel pressure. WARNING: Keep all open flames away from the area you do this test as fuel may be released into the air
	Bad ignition switch, electronic control module, or PCM fuse or relay	Check ignition, electronic control module (ECM), and PCM fuses and relays. Replace any failed fuses. *(Project 17: Test and Replace Fuses)*
	No spark	Check for spark at spark plug while cranking engine. If you see fat blue spark on spark plug, your engine is most likely not getting fuel. Go to Fuel System Troubleshooting chart. If no spark, check several different plugs to be sure the problem is not with one spark plug only. If only one plug lacks spark, suggest replacing spark plug wires and (if your car has one) distributor cap If several plugs are without spark, check all fuses and relays (see your owner's manual). If fuses test good, take in to your mechanic for diagnosis. *(Project 17: Test and Replace Fuses)*
	Check main power/ASD (auto shutdown) relays	Try replacement relay
ONE OR BOTH HEADLIGHTS ARE OUT	Headlight bulb burned out	Check headlight bulbs and replace bulbs that have broken filaments. *(Project 20: Replace Headlight Bulb)*

ELECTRICAL SYSTEM TROUBLESHOOTING

PROBLEM	PROBABLE CAUSES	ACTION TO REPAIR
BOTH HEADLIGHTS AND RUNNING LIGHTS OUT	Check headlight/running light fuses/relays	Replace any failed bulbs, fuses, or relays
	Faulty connection/ headlight switch	Check, clean, and reset headlight switch connector under dash
NO HIGH/LOW BEAMS	Loose connection in harness connector	Check high/low beam switch and connector/harness
NO BRAKE LIGHTS	Faulty/misadjusted brake light switch	Check connections under dash at brake light switch
		Use jumper to connect wires together for test; brake lights should illuminate
		Adjust brake light switch. In most cases, push switch up toward pedal linkage, then step firmly on brake pedal
	Bad connection in harness	Check harness/connection to brake lights
NO TURN SIGNALS OR EMERGENCY FLASHERS	Bad relay or flasher unit	Check relay/flasher unit; try replacement unit if needed
NO INTERIOR OR DASH LIGHTS	Faulty door switch	Older vehicles—check plunger on door frame. Does plunger extend with door open and ground circuit?
		Newer vehicles—door switch is built into door latching mechanism inside door. Try spraying aerosol lubricant down push-button lock opening/latch opening to lube latch mechanism. Must remove interior door trim to access latch/switch
	Faulty courtesy/gem module	Check fuse/relay module, usually under the dash (Project 17: Test and Replace Fuses)
INTERIOR LIGHT OUT	Faulty lamp, socket, or ground	Check/replace bulb, check for voltage to ground at socket
NO HEATER/AC FAN	Faulty relay/fuse/control module	Check fuses/relays. (Project 17: Test and Replace Fuses)
	Faulty fan motor	Test by using jumper wire from Bat + to positive + terminal on blower motor. Motor should be run on high speed
HEATER FAN ONLY RUNS ON HIGH SETTING	Faulty heater fan resistor block	Check and replace heater fan resistor block, usually on heater box on firewall or under dash on passenger side
ACCESSORIES NOT WORKING (stereo, rear window defroster, power windows, power door locks, power seat, power antenna, power trunk/door, hatch release, power sunroof)	Bad fuse or relay	Check and replace appropriate fuse and relay
	Ground connection faulty	Check for bad ground to circuit

Project 9

Change Plug Wires and Plugs

TALENT:	2
TIME:	30–45 minutes
TOOLS:	Socket wrench with deep-well sockets and long extender
COST:	$35–$50
TIP:	Add a dab of anti-seize compound to threads to prevent plugs from getting stuck. Be sure they thread in and turn smoothly. Do not use the wrench to force a resistant plug as you'll destroy the thread.

1 Installing plugs and wires is relatively straightforward on a vehicle like this Honda, where access is good. Some V-6 engines in front-wheel-drive vehicles can be very difficult to access on the back side and may require tipping the engine forward to change those spark plugs. If the plug wires are thin like regular wire, the vehicle has coil-on-plug ignition and wire replacement is not routine maintenance.

2 The plug wire pulls off at the spark plug end. Grasp and pull at the boot around the spark plug, not the wire itself. It's always a good idea to use compressed air (from your compressor or a can of compressed air from an electronics store) to blow any dirt and debris out of the spark plug well before removing the plug. Most plugs today come gapped from the supplier, unlike plugs on older cars that required gapping by the installer. It's never a bad idea to check the gap with an inexpensive spark plug gapping tool from the auto parts store.

3 The spark plug can then be removed with a deep-well socket.

4 The plug wire also pulls off at the distributor end (if there's a distributor). Be sure to keep track of which wire comes off which connection. Installing them in the wrong place will mix-up the engine's firing order, causing poor performance and possible damage. An easy way to remember is to mark each connection with a small piece of masking tape identifying which plug it goes to.

Replace Distributor Cap and Rotor

TALENT:	3
TIME:	15–30 minutes
TOOLS:	None, or screwdriver/ socket wrench
COST:	$25–$50
TIP:	Some rotors screw on; some push on. If it won't pull off, locate and remove the retaining screw.

1 Remove the plug wires as in Project 9 (Change Plug Wires and Plugs), keeping track of which one went on which connection. Then release the fasteners securing the distributor cap. Older vehicles typically used clips that could be popped off with your thumb or a small screw driver. This Honda's cap is mounted with small bolts.

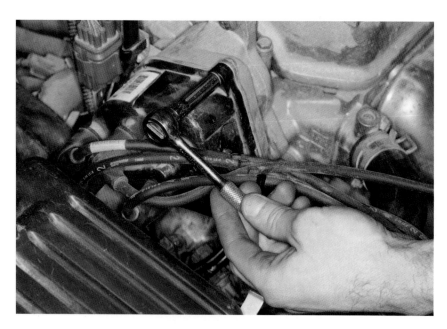

2 The rotor is the round part under the cap.

3 Some rotors pull off. This Honda's is secured with a screw to the distributor shaft. Remove the screw to lift off the rotor.

Note: If the tip of the rotor isn't burned or worn, you might be able to clean and polish it with a piece of Scotch-Brite, or steel wool, and reuse it.

Reverse these steps to fit the new rotor and cap.

Project 11
Test Alternator

TALENT:	3
TIME:	15 minutes
TOOLS:	Voltmeter
COST:	$25–50
TIP:	If the battery won't charge, check for a loose or disconnected wire to the alternator, and check battery connections.

1 You can test your alternator with a voltmeter, a handy tool for checking many parts of your electrical system. First test the battery voltage with the engine off. This will display the battery's available voltage. It should be about 12.5 volts.

2 Start the engine and test the battery again. If the voltmeter shows more voltage than the battery displayed with the engine off—hopefully 13–15 volts—the alternator is working.

Project 12
Replace Alternator

TALENT: 4

TIME: 30–60 minutes

TOOLS: Screwdriver, socket wrench, extender(s)

COST: $75–$200

TIP: Have a store test the old alternater to confirm that it's bad. You will typically get a core refund when you buy your new alternator, so bring the old one to the parts store.

1 Disconnect the negative battery cable. Remove the alternator belt by releasing the tension and lifting it off the alternator pulley. The tensioner may be on the alternator itself, as with the Dodge in Project 29 (Replace Water Pump), or it may come from a spring-loaded or adjustable pulley applying tension to the belt (as described in Project 8, Replace Serpentine Belt).

The routing of the belt is shown here.

2 Disconnect the wires, which often include both a plug and a bolt-on connection.

3 Remove the bolts securing the alternator case to the engine and any brackets. This Dodge Dakota has one bolt parallel to the alternator shaft (shown here). It has another perpendicular to it (shown, loosened, in the top photo). Mounting bolts have many configurations but the basic steps for changing an alternator are the same.

4 The bolt is shown back in place. As you put the belt back on, make sure the ribs on the belt align with the pulley correctly. The tension is set automatically by the tensioner.

5 Even with the bolts removed, the alternator may be a snug fit. You may need to wiggle it back and forth to move it and possibly to lever it with a long screwdriver or metal bar. Pry slowly and carefully, and distribute the force evenly along the stuck surfaces so it doesn't jam.

Project 13

Project 13
Replace Starter

TALENT:	3–5 (depending on location and obstructions)
TIME:	30–90 minutes
TOOLS:	Socket wrench, combination wrench(s)
COST:	$100–$250
TIP:	You will get a core refund for your old starter, as with your old alternator.

1 Before performing any electrical work—or any work in the engine bay, for that matter—disconnect the negative battery cable.

Always wear gloves when working with batteries.

2 The starter motor is usually bolted to the transmission end of the engine and has a drive gear or pinion that reaches into the space where the engine and transmission join, called the bell housing. The starter on this Toyota Camry lies just underneath the orange handle by the radiator hose. When activated, this gear engages a toothed ring gear mounted on the flywheel on a stick shift car or the flex plate on an automatic. By spinning the flywheel, or flex plate, the starter cranks the engine.

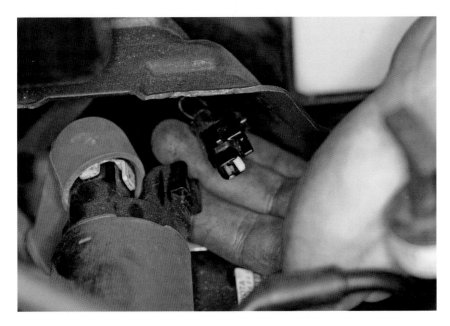

3 Disconnect the electrical cables from the starter. They may just need to be unplugged, or they may be bolted to a threaded stud.

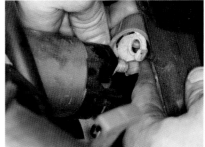

4 Unbolt the starter from the engine and pull it back out of its recess.

5 Space is tight on this Camry; getting the starter out required pushing on the big, black air box to create just a tiny extra bit of clearance. The starter could then be lifted free from under the radiator hose. Note any shims or spacers used between the starter motor and its mount to control or adjust the pinion gear's engagement with the ring gear. If there are any, make sure you put them back when you reinstall the starter.

Installation is the reverse of removal. Reattaching the negative battery cable is your final step.

Project 14
Clean Battery Posts

TALENT: 1

TIME: 15 minutes

TOOLS: Battery post cleaner or wire brush, commercial cleaner or baking soda

COST: $0–$10

TIP: Wear old clothes and gloves whenever working with a car battery, as acid readily makes holes in clothing.

1 Battery posts, terminals, and cables can—and usually do—corrode over time, leaving a white crusty substance. This substance interferes with current flow and should be removed.

Wear safety glasses and gloves when working with your battery. Wash your hands and your clothes as soon as you finish the job.

2 Detach the battery cables, negative connection first.

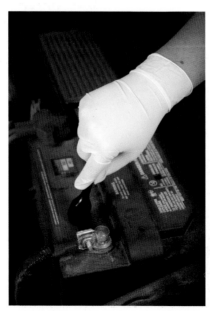

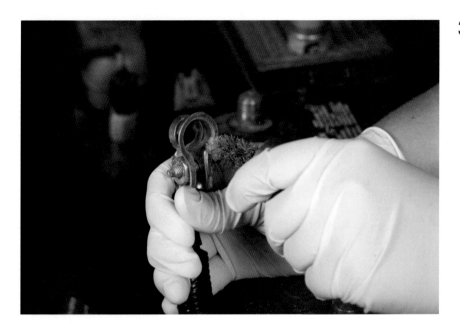

3 Using a wire brush, clean the corrosion from the battery cable and terminal.

4 An inexpensive battery post cleaner has both a regular brush and post brush.

5 Clean the posts by placing this over each one and rotating it back and forth to remove corrosion.

CLEAN BATTERY POSTS

6 Once the posts are well cleaned, use a solution of baking soda and water with a bucket and sponge, or a splash of diet soft drink to cleanse and neutralize the acid and corrosion.

Don't forget to remove corrosion from the battery support and battery tray.

7 Auto stores also sell aerosol sprays and felt O-rings treated with an anti-corrosive agent that you can place underneath the battery leads to inhibit future corrosion.

8 Reinstall the battery cables. Positive first, then negative.

Project 15

Check Battery Electrolyte

TALENT:	1
TIME:	5 minutes
TOOLS:	Tester
COST:	$10
TIP:	Wear old clothes and gloves and clean up any battery acid that spills to minimize corrosion.

1 Some batteries are permanently sealed. Others, like this one, have caps that allow you to check the battery's electrolyte level and strength. Gently pry the caps up and lift them off. Set them on a paper towel to absorb any electrolyte.

Wear safety glasses and gloves, and wash your hands and clothes after testing.

2 Shine a flashlight into each cell to determine whether the electrolyte level is above the top of the plates. If not, add just enough distilled water to cover the plates. Now insert the tester into the electrolyte and draw it into test cylinder. The floating disc or balls indicate the state of charge retained by that cell.

Replace Battery

TALENT:	2
TIME:	15–30 minutes
TOOLS:	Small wrench for cables; socket wrench with extender may be necessary for bracket bolt
COST:	$50–$150
TIP:	If you store a vehicle, periodically charge the battery, or use a trickle charger to keep it alive.

1 Again, make sure you're wearing safety glasses and gloves. Disconnect and pull aside the negative battery cable. Do the same with the positive battery cable.

2 Disconnect and remove any battery mounting brackets or hardware, which may be attached at the bottom (lower left), as it is here, or may run across the top of the battery.

3 Lift the battery free, keeping it level to avoid possibility of spilling acid. Any inexpensive battery lifting strap (available at auto parts stores) makes removing a top terminal battery much easier.

If your battery has top terminals but you use the side ones, as shown here, keep the top terminals capped to eliminate the risk that a metal tool or part could short across them and create a fire hazard.

Test and Replace Fuses

TALENT: 2

TIME: 15–30 minutes

TOOLS: Fuse(s), tester

COST: $25–$40

TIP: Your owner's manual should explain which fuse goes where and controls what. Relays, which are boxes or cylinders plugged into the fuse box, can also fail, rendering a component (such as the fuel pump, turn signal, or air conditioner) inoperable.

1 See your owner's manual for fuse locations and functions. An inexpensive test light is the easiest way to check a fuse's condition. Clip the test light's negative lead to the battery's negative cable, then touch the tip to each leg, or end of the fuse, in turn. On plastic blade-style fuses, there's a little slot or opening at the top of each leg; that's where to touch with the probe. If power is available at the fuse and the fuse is good, the test light will glow on both sides. If the fuse is bad, it will only glow on the power or battery side of the fuse. Another way is to remove the fuse and check it visually. The wire in a bad fuse will be broken.

2 To remove a blade-style fuse, grip it on each side, and pull it free. An inexpensive plastic fuse puller, available at parts stores, makes this job a bit easier.

To remove the older style glass BUSS fuse, use an inexpensive fuse puller to grasp the glass tube near one end, pull it loose, and then pull the fuse free.

3 Replace a fuse by pressing it back into the proper slots in the fuse box

If a fuse is blown, there's a reason. It could be either a momentary short circuit or the circuit is drawing too much current. Never try to fix a blown fuse by installing a higher amperage fuse. Doing so is an invitation to overheated wiring and a potential electrical fire.

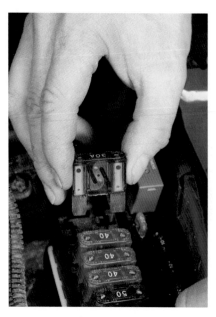

4 If the fuse is good, the metal connection (S-shaped on this fuse) between the two contacts will be visibly intact. If the fuse is blown, this connection would be burnt through and open. Sometimes a fuse that looks good will not work correctly because it isn't properly seated in the fuse box. For this reason, a test light is a better indicator of a fuse's behavior than a visual inspection.

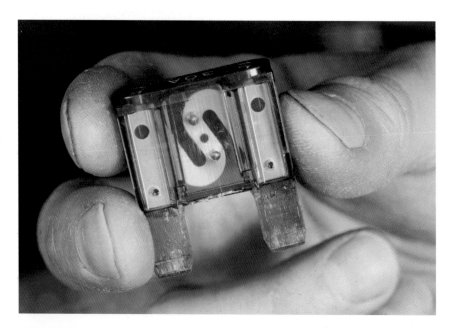

Project 18
Replace Taillight Bulb

TALENT: 1–2

TIME: 15–30 minutes

TOOLS: Socket wrench/
screwdriver

COST: $5–$10

TIP: Check the bulb you
remove to ensure that its
filament is broken; a bad
fuse, relay, or loose
connection can also shut
down your taillight.

1 Find the wiring and harness. It may
lie behind material lining the trunk.

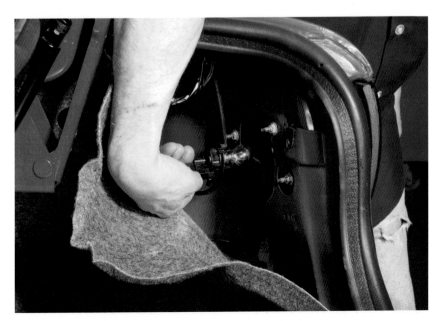

2 Most modern vehicles utilize a light
socket that locks into place with a
twist. To remove it, grip the
plastic base the wiring runs into, and
turn it counterclockwise. You can
then slide the bulb out of the taillight
lens assembly.

3 Grip the bulb at its plastic base and pull it out of the socket. The light brown grease in this picture is dielectric grease, which improves electrical connections and resists water. Do not use regular grease for this purpose.

4 Insert the new bulb, slip the socket back into the taillight lens assembly, and twist it into place. Any auto parts store or dealership has the bulb you need. Many of them are now standardized.

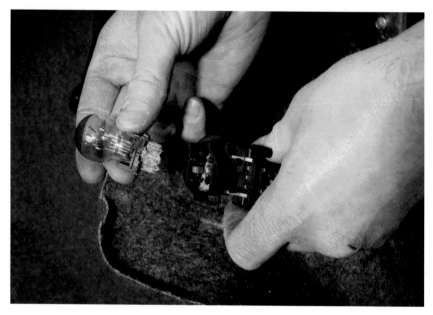

Project 19

Replace Taillight Lens

TALENT:	2
TIME:	15 minutes
TOOLS:	Socket wrench
COST:	$20–$50
TIP:	If there is any water behind the lens, dry it out; if the seal around the lens is damaged, replace it (a new seal may come with the lens assembly).

1 A cracked lens will eventually suffer water damage and become clouded.

2 Expose the wiring/harness by pulling back any trunk lining material in the way. Remove the taillight bulb by twisting the socket and pulling it free, as described in Project 18 (Replace Taillight Bulb). Now loosen the bolts securing the taillight lens assembly.

3 Hold the lens assembly as you remove the last securing nut or bolt, then pull the assembly free. Modern cars typically incorporate the lens into an assembly, like this Chevrolet's. You replace the complete assembly rather than just the red lens; that's why they cost so much more.

Reassemble by reversing these steps.

REPLACE TAILLIGHT LENS

Project 20

Project 20

Replace Headlight Bulb

TALENT: 2

TIME: 15–30 minutes

TOOLS: Socket wrench (possibly side cutters to remove body clip if present)

COST: $3 and up

TIP: Be careful not to upset the headlight aiming screws.

1 Some headlight bulbs are accessible from the engine bay and require removing nothing but the bulb fixture itself. With this Chevy Cavalier, we need to remove a plastic shield across the top of the front of the engine compartment.

2 You can use a side cutter pliers to remove some body clips; use it as a wedge and lever, rather than squeezing the handles together to cut. This reveals the headlight housing mounting bolts.

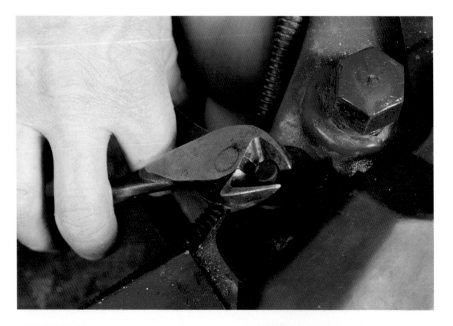

3 Remove the bolts securing the headlight housing.

4 Now pull the housing forward to expose the electrical harness.

5 Rotate the locking ring or socket counterclockwise and pull the headlight bulb free of the headlight housing. Now unplug the bulb.

Plug the new bulb in and reverse the removal procedure.

Don't touch a halogen headlight bulb except at the plastic base. Oil from your fingers on the glass can cause the bulb to fail prematurely.

Project 21

Replace Turn-Signal Bulb

TALENT: 1–2

TIME: 15–30 minutes

TOOLS: Combination or socket wrench

COST: $5–$10

TIP: Check for a broken filament; if unbroken, check fuse, wiring, and relay for source of signal failure.

1 Turn-signal lamp replacement is much like replacing a taillight. For clearance, some vehicles, like this Ford Ranger, require that you remove the turn-signal housing from the body to access the bulb. The housing may combine nuts and bolts with fasteners that press into a clip.

2 The Ranger's turn-signal housing requires removing only one bolt.

3 Pull the housing free.

4 Turn the socket counterclockwise and pull it from the housing.

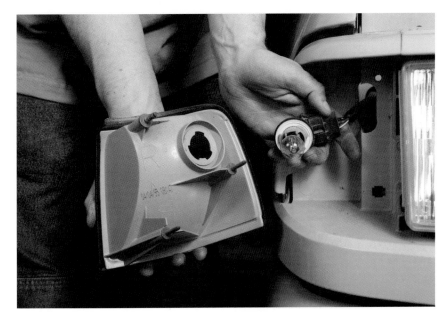

5 The bulb then pulls free from the fixture.

Insert new bulb and reassemble in the reverse order. A small amount of dielectric grease (not regular grease) will aid the connection and repel moisture.

Project 22

Project 22
Replace Back-Up Light

TALENT: 1–2

TIME: 15–30 minutes

TOOLS: Screwdriver

COST: $5–$10

TIP: Check for water behind lens; dry and check seal if present.

1 The reverse, or back-up, lights often reside in the same housings as the tails and turn-signal lights, particularly on trucks.

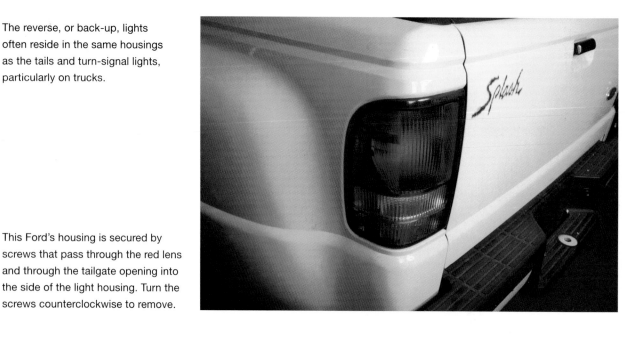

2 This Ford's housing is secured by screws that pass through the red lens and through the tailgate opening into the side of the light housing. Turn the screws counterclockwise to remove.

3 The housing then pulls free of its opening.

4 To remove the back-up light socket from the housing, turn it counter-clockwise and pull it out.

5 Grip the bulb at its plastic base and pull it out of the socket.

Insert new bulb and reassemble in the reverse order.

Chapter 5

Cooling System

 WARNING!

KEY CONCEPT

 OLD SCHOOL TECH

MAINTENANCE TIP

TOMORROW'S TECH

MONEY-SAVING TIP

Internal combustion engines produce power by burning the fuel to create tremendous heat and pressure, which is converted to mechanical power to move the vehicle. And for all the wonderful efficiency of modern engines, they are only about 80 percent efficient in converting the energy in the fuel into useful power. Said differently, engines produce more heat than they can convert into power, thus the need for some type of cooling system to control operating temperatures and prevent overheating.

Two types of cooling systems have been utilized over the decades: air and water. Ultimately, all of the excess heat produced by an engine must be dissipated into the atmosphere. Engines in some vehicles, like the flat four-cylinder powerplant in the iconic Volkswagen Beetle, were cooled directly by airflow over the cylinder heads and block. There was no separate cooling system to service, no coolant to drain and flush, no thermostat to change, and no water pump to leak and fail, just a belt-driven fan to blow air over the engine. But for all the simplicity, light weight, and reliability of air-cooled engines in automobiles, they tend to suffer from higher operating temperatures with greater losses in performance and fuel economy. And because there's no coolant, they're not as efficient in supplying heat to keep the cabin and occupants toasted warm.

Air cooling is still popular with smaller engines found in lawn and garden equipment.

The vast majority of motor vehicles feature closed liquid cooling systems. The water pump circulates the coolant through the cylinder block and cylinder heads, to absorb and carry away the excess combustion heat and to the radiator, which exchanges the heat into the atmospheric air moving past its cooling fins and cores.

To help the efficiency of the liquid cooling system, it is pressurized and thermostatically controlled. By operating the system at higher pressures, typically 7–16 psi, the boiling point of the water-based coolant rises. By raising the boiling point to the 250 degrees Fahrenheit or a higher level, the coolant won't boil and loose efficiency at normal engine operating temperatures of 180–230 degrees Fahrenheit. The pressure is controlled by the pressure cap on the radiator or recovery tank.

COOLING SYSTEM TROUBLESHOOTING

PROBLEM	PROBABLE CAUSES	ACTION TO REPAIR
LOW COOLANT LIGHT ILLUMINATED	Coolant is low	Check coolant level in recovery tank/radiator; add coolant. Remember: Do not open radiator cap unless engine is completely cool
	Monitor coolant level in recovery tank weekly/daily to determine rate of coolant loss	If loss is more than nominal, have cooling system professionally checked
COOLANT PUDDLES UNDERNEATH CAR	Leak in system	Determine what part of cooling system is directly above spot. Inspect that area of engine compartment for leaks If leak is from hose connection, tighten hose clamp Check for leakage/wetness on bottom of water pump If water pump is leaking, replace water pump. (Project 29: Replace Water Pump) Monitor rate of leak, as above
COOLANT TEMPERATURE WARNING LIGHT ILLUMINATED	Pull safely off road and stop engine as soon as possible. **WARNING:** Continuing to drive with overheated engine can lead to serious engine damage	Let engine cool 30 minutes or more; restart. If temperature light goes out, drive to service station. If not, have car towed.
ENGINE OVERHEATING TO THE POINT THAT SMOKE OR STEAM COMES FROM UNDERNEATH THE HOOD	Coolant leak, low coolant, blocked or failing radiator	If smoke/steam is coming from under the hood, do not open the hood! Wait for engine to cool (at least 30 minutes), then open hood carefully. Check coolant level in recovery tank; add coolant if necessary. Look for signs of leakage (puddles of green coolant or wet hoses or connections); if you identify source of leak as hose or connection, replace hose or tighten connection. Test drive car to see if steam returns; if not, carefully monitor coolant level over next few weeks. If steam returns, let car cool, refill with antifreeze, and take in to mechanic for repair. (Project 23: Check/Fill Coolant; Project 26: Replace Radiator Hose)
VIBRATION UNDER HOOD	Bad water pump drive belt	Check water pump drive belt for frays, cracks, or other damage; if water pump belt is damaged, replace it. (Project 29: Replace Water Pump) Check radiator for coolant flow/blockage Check grille/frontal opening for air restriction to radiator

COOLING SYSTEM TROUBLESHOOTING

PROBLEM	PROBABLE CAUSES	ACTION TO REPAIR
TEMPERATURE GAUGE READS ABOVE NORMAL AND/OR CLIMBING	Coolant leak, low coolant, blocked or failing heater. NOTE: Once the gauge hits the maximum reading or red zone, you are heading for an overheat with steam rising out of the hood. If that happens, see **Engine Overheating** section above	When your temperature gauge reads above normal, you can take the following measures to slow down the overheating process: Turn on heater to "high" and fan to "high" to dissipate more engine heat; pull to safe location, shift to neutral; run engine at fast idle to increase coolant circulation
	Radiator fan not functioning	Check/listen for radiator fan operation
	Water pump failing	Check water pump belt
	Leaking coolant from hose connection	When engine is safely cooled down, identify area of leak and tighten hose clamp. *(Project 26: Replace Radiator Hose)*
	Cooling system hose ruptured	Remove, shorten, and reinstall hose. *(Project 26: Replace Radiator Hose)*
	Punctured radiator	If radiator is punctured, add stop-leak product
		Pressure test the system. NOTE: Do not loosen/remove radiator cap until engine is fully cooled down. *(Project 30: Pressure Test System)*
		Refill cooling system with water or anti-freeze mix
		Replace radiator. *(Project 27: Replace Your Radiator)*
NO HEAT FROM HEATER	Low coolant level	Check coolant level in recovery tank; after engine is cool, check coolant level in radiator. *(Project 23: Check/Fill Coolant)*
	Thermostat is stuck open (coolant never heats up enough to provide good heat in the car)	Replace thermostat. *(Project 25: Change Radiator Cap and Thermostat)*
		NOTE: Do not loosen/remove radiator cap until engine is fully cooled down
LOUD ROARING SOUND UNDER HOOD	Hydraulic fan clutch seized/failed	Replace fan clutch
GREASY FILM ON INSIDE OF WINDSHIELD, BITTERSWEET SMELL INSIDE CAR; WET CARPET IN PASSENGER FLOORWELL	Coolant leak from heater core	Add stop-leak product to radiator for temporary repair. You will eventually need to find bad connection and fix, or replace heater core entirely

Project 23
Check/Fill Coolant

TALENT:	1
TIME:	5 minutes
TOOLS:	Coolant, funnel
COST:	$10
TIP:	Pay attention to your engine temperature gauge and stop immediately at any sign of overheating. An overheated engine can suffer damage like a warped cylinder head, which can lead to other problems, such as a blown head gasket.

1 Contemporary radiators typically have a separate overflow reservoir indicating the proper coolant level. On some vehicles, coolant can be checked via the radiator cap when the engine is completely cold. Some manufacturers may use a sealed system with no accessible radiator cap.

Never loosen the radiator cap when the engine is hot—scalding coolant will spray out.

2 To check coolant level in the radiator when the engine is cool, press down on the radiator cap, rotate it counterclockwise two positions, and remove it.

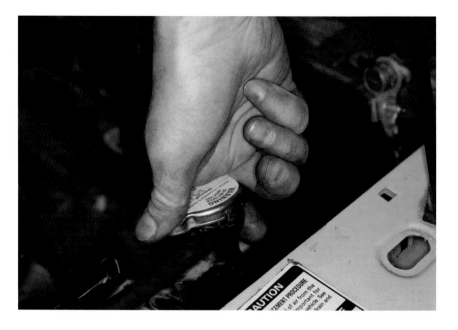

3 You should see coolant through the open filler neck. If you've just replaced the radiator or a hose or have flushed the radiator, you will need to fill it here.

4 If you're refilling an empty cooling system, mix equal parts coolant and water in a clean container (for coolant that is not pre-mixed), then pour from that. See Project 24 on checking fluid concentration.

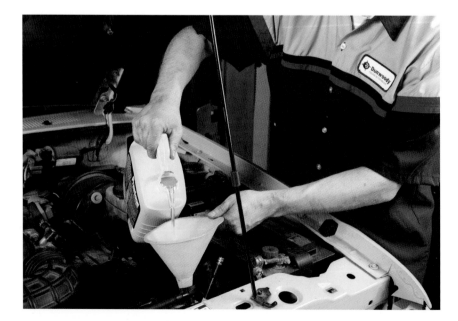

5 An inexpensive tool some mechanics use to fill radiators features a reservoir that attaches like a radiator cap at the filler neck. Pour coolant until it fills the bottom of the reservoir and run the engine with the tool attached. Add coolant if the reservoir empties. When no more coolant flows into the radiator, insert a plunger-style plug to seal the reservoir, then remove the tool and install the radiator cap.

6 Your radiator has an overflow reservoir. If pressure gets too high in the radiator, the cap will release pressure and expel some coolant into the reservoir. As the system cools down and pressure drops, it will draw some coolant back into the radiator. This overflow container should always have some coolant in it. A marker will indicate where the level should be when the system is cold or hot. If the reservoir is low, add coolant until the level is just above the COLD fill line.

Note: Your cooling system is filled with the antifreeze concentration the manufacturer recommends, usually a 50/50 coolant/water mix. (See Project 24, Check Fluid Concentration.)

Some coolants come premixed, so read the label. Use a funnel and pour slowly to avoid a spill. If you've drained the cooling system, it will contain air that must be displaced with coolant. To do so, grab and squeeze a radiator hose a couple times as you fill.

Be patient, you'll need to add coolant slowly to allow air to escape and the system to fill completely.

CHECK/FILL COOLANT

Check Fluid Concentration

TALENT:	1
TIME:	5 minutes
TOOLS:	Tester
COST:	$10
TIP:	Some coolant comes pre-mixed; read the label carefully.

1 When the engine is cold, remove the radiator cap. Squeeze the rubber bulb on the antifreeze tester. Insert the tube into the radiator filler neck and release the bulb.

2 Draw coolant out until it fills the plastic reservoir and read the indicator. It will show the freezing point of your coolant mixture. This point must be below the lowest temperatures experienced in your area. If the strength is too weak, add pure antifreeze coolant; if it's too strong, add distilled water. Then retest.

Change Radiator Cap and Thermostat

TALENT:	3
TIME:	30–60 minutes
TOOLS:	Combination or socket wrench
COST:	$20–$30
TIP:	Caps come in different pressure ratings. Be sure you get the correct one for your vehicle.

1 Radiator caps are spring-loaded to maintain a certain amount of pressure in the system. When cooling system pressure is too high, the spring-loaded seal is forced upward, releasing pressure and allowing coolant to escape into the overflow reservoir. It's not a bad idea to replace your radiator cap every few years, or according to manufacturer recommendations, to be sure it seals and functions properly. To remove—with the engine cold, of course—push firmly down with the palm of your gloved hand and twist the cap counterclockwise.

2 On most vehicles, the thermostat is located where the top radiator hose connects to its housing. Removing the thermostat housing will typically release some coolant, so position a drain pan accordingly. Better yet, drain the radiator down to a level below the thermostat housing.

3 Use the correct socket or open-end wrench to reach and loosen the thermostat housing bolts.

4 When you remove the housing, note it's orientation on the engine.

5 You may need a screwdriver to coax the thermostat loose if it sticks. See how the inner, or engine, side—which contains the temperature-sensitive element—looks different from the outside. Don't install the new one upside down as it will not work properly.

6 The gasket may be an attached ring around the thermostat itself, as it is here, or a separate sheet cut to match the housing. Clean off the traces of the old gasket. Install the new thermostat with gasket just as the old one sat, and tighten the bolts. Run the engine and check for leaks.

Project 26

Replace Radiator Hose

TALENT: 3

TIME: 30–60 minutes

TOOLS: Screwdriver or pliers, depending on hose clamp type

COST: $20–$40

TIP: Replace clamps at the same time. See Project 24 for instructions on how to drain the system.

1 A radiator hose that leaks or shows signs of damage (a bulge, splits, hardened, checking, or cracking rubber) must be replaced. If you've driven the vehicle to the auto parts store, compare the replacement hose with the old one before you drive away. If you have a second vehicle, take the old hose with you to the store to make sure you get the right replacement.

An upper radiator hose can typically be changed without draining the cooling system, though some coolant will leak out. Replacing a lower hose will require draining the coolant first. Place a drain pan below the hose. Remove any component blocking access to the hose. Here, we've removed the air intake (explained in Project 22, Replace Radiator).

2 Remove the hose clamps from each end by squeezing the two ends together. If the clamp is the screw/worm gear type, use a screwdriver or socket that fits the screw/bolt head and turn it counter-clockwise to loosen.

3 Twist the hose to pull it off the outlet.

4 If it sticks, you can usually free it by sliding a flat-blade screwdriver between the hose and outlet. To install the new hose, slip the clamp for each end over the new hose, push/twist the hose onto the outlets and secure the clamps.

Refill Radiator as covered in Project 24.

Project 27
Replace Your Radiator

TALENT: 5

TIME: 60–120 minutes

TOOLS: Pliers/hose clamp tool,
           socket wrench,
           screwdriver, extender,
           side cutter (for body clips)

COST: $150–$300

TIP: A doable home project
           on trucks, SUVs, and other
           vehicles with relatively
           roomy engine bays.

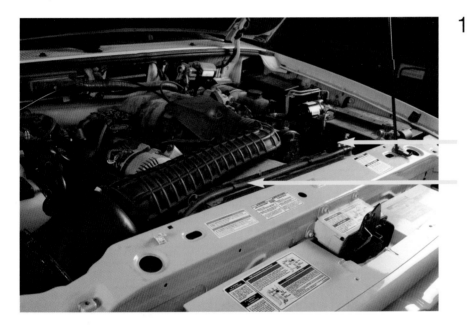

1 This Ford Ranger has a typical modern engine bay. The radiator mounts at the front. The radiator cap lies to the right in this photo, with an overflow hose running from the filler neck and across the top to the recovery tank. The thick pipe with the grid pattern is an air intake for the fuel system. Both the radiator and induction components are easier to remove than appears at first glance. Your vehicle's radiator may not be obstructed by an intake. If not, skip ahead to draining the radiator and unbolting it.

2 Like most vehicle radiators, this Ford Ranger's bolts to the front of the truck. Behind it, and bolted to it, is a fan shroud. Both the radiator and the shroud in this vehicle are bolted only at the top; the bottom is secured by a simple flange on each side that drops into a groove or slot.

3 There are two ways to drain a radiator. One is to disconnect the lower hose. Since removing the hose drains the radiator faster, and is required to replace the radiator, that's what we did.

4 The other way to drain a radiator, where available, is to open a petcock, a T-shaped valve on the lower part of the radiator that opens like a faucet.

Coolant gets very hot; do not open the radiator cap or loosen a hose until the engine is cold.

5 Modern hose clamps are spring steel that secure the end of the hose onto a short tubular outlet on the radiator or other hose connection. To remove the clamp, squeeze the two ends together and slide it back.

6 Another way to release a hose clamp is with this special tool, which grabs the tab on each side of the clamp and pulls them together. This tool has a long flexible cable, so it can reach into tight spaces.

Place a large pail or drain pan below the hose. Twist the hose end back and forth to pull it off. Be careful not to flex or crack the outlet where it joins the radiator. The coolant will rush out, so direct the hose into your container quickly to avoid spills.

☠ Coolant is toxic to humans and pets. Keep coolant containers sealed and out of children's and pets' reach. If coolant spills, clean it up quickly, either by hosing the area off thoroughly with water or mopping it up with shop towels.

7 While the coolant drains, remove any parts blocking access to the radiator. First will be the air intake, which blocks access to the radiator bolts and upper hose. The Ranger intake is secured at each end with a clamp. Along its length it has two electronic sensor attachments and an air line. The sensors unclip and the air line simply pulls out. Electronic sensors often have a little catch on them with a slotted tab that clicks onto a small nub. To unclip, pull the tab back or push it in to clear the locking nub then pull the two halves apart.

8 The engine end of the air intake mounts with a circular clip attached by a vertical screw or bolt. This one has a bolt-style head that is also slotted, so you can loosen it with a screwdriver, socket, or wrench. There is a clip just like this at the other end too, which attaches to the air filter housing. You may not need to remove that one, as separating the air filter housing may allow you to remove the parts.

9 The air intake sensor pulls apart once the locking tab (just left of thumb in photo) is lifted.

10 The second sensor also pulls apart; this time the catch releases with a press of the index finger, as shown.

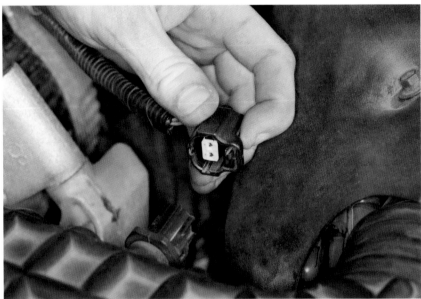

11 The air line pulls out.

Project 28
Flush Cooling System

TALENT: 3

TIME: 45–60 minutes

TOOLS: Razor blade, screwdriver

COST: $15–$20

TIP: Flush cooling system every two years, or as recommended in your owner's manual.

Over time, rust, scale and deposits will accumulate in your engine's cooling system. The way to clear these out and maintain your cooling system's maximum efficiency is to flush the system—that is, run water through it. In this project, we will show you how to install an inline flushing receptor. This allows you to flush your cooling system with a garden hose.

1 Find a return line from the heating system or heater core with enough straight length to accommodate the special fitting. Ask a mechanic or check a service manual to ensure that you have the correct hose.

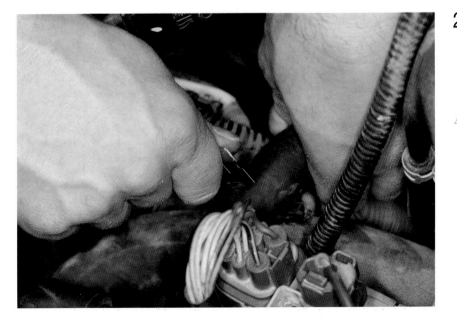

2 Place a drain pain beneath the hose to catch any coolant. With a razor blade, knife, or other sharp cutter, make a straight cut through the hose.

⚠ Handle sharp tools carefully. Never push any tool—razor blade, knife, cutter, screwdriver, etc.—toward your other hand or someone else's.

3 Slide the hose clamps over each end of the cut hose and insert the receptor that fits the hose (the kit includes several).

4 Move the hose clamps into position over the fittings and tighten them. Attach the hose to the fitting when you're ready to flush the radiator. (Otherwise, keep the cap in place.) The fitting remains in the system for future flushing.

5 Attach the radiator nozzle to the filler neck. You may need to tape it if it does not snap in. Place a large bucket or drain pan in front of the nozzle and run the hose to flush the system.

Project 29
Replace Water Pump

TALENT: 5

TIME: 60–120 minutes

TOOLS: Socket wrench, combination wrench, screwdriver, pliers

COST: $25–$75

TIP: Keep track of bolt locations, as some may be longer than others.

1 The water pump draws coolant from the bottom of the radiator and pumps it through the engine. If the fan is driven by the engine (electric fans aren't), the water pump is typically on the other end of the same shaft.

The water pump is located behind the fan.

2 Disconnect the negative battery lead. Make sure the engine is cold and drain the cooling system. To do this, disconnect the lower radiator hose at the radiator or open the petcock, if the radiator has one, with a drain pan placed below. You will most likely need to disconnect the upper radiator hose as well, and shift it out of the way (See Project 24).

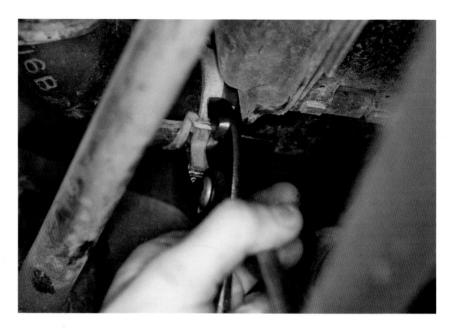

3 For better access, remove the fan shroud, first disconnecting the radiator overflow hose if it is attached to the shroud. The shroud will be bolted to the radiator or support at the top, while the bottom will either be bolted or secured via a flange that drops into a slot.

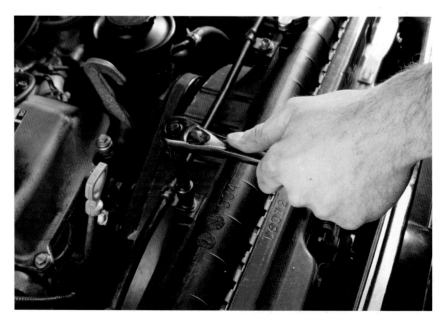

4 This Toyota Tacoma's shroud is split at the midpoint. The bottom lip must be unclipped (the clips pull off) and removed so the shroud will clear the fan when you lift it out.

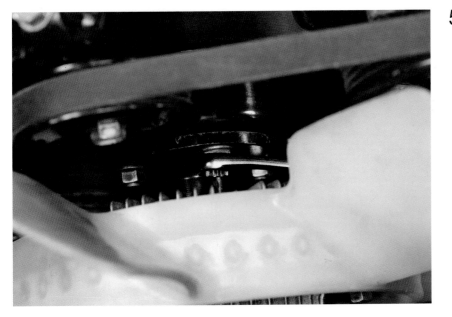

5 Leave the water pump drive belt in place while loosening the bolts securing the pulley to the water pump. The belt will help prevent the pulley from rotating as you loosen the bolts. Don't remove bolts until relieving the tension on belt.

6 The power steering pulley is in our way here, so we will remove it. In order to do that, you must release the belt tension. On this Tacoma, the tensioner is a bolt that loosens with a wrench turned counterclockwise. Serpentine belt tensioners often involve a pulley on a spring-loaded arm. (See Project 8, Replace Serpentine Belt.) The water pump drive belt is just visible here below the mechanic's thumb.

7 Release the tension on the water pump drive belt. On the Tacoma, this is done by loosening two bolts on the alternator: the first clamping the alternator to its bracket; and the second, shown here above mechanic's thumb, allowing the alternator to swing in or out to adjust tension on the belt.

8 Now remove the water pump pulley along with the fan (where attached).

9 Here is the water pump with its pulley removed and the four studs that hold the pulley and fan.

10 To remove the water pump, remove all bolts holding it to the engine.

11 Remove the pump and gasket. Your new water pump will come with a new gasket.

Installation is the reverse of removal. Remember to attach the lower radiator hose or close the petcock valve. If the coolant you drained was fresh and drained into a clean pan, you can pour it back into the radiator once you've replaced the pump. If not, refill the system with fresh coolant, as described in Project 24. Remove all traces of old gasket from water pump and block.

Project 30

Pressure Test System

TALENT:	2–3
TIME:	15 minutes
TOOLS:	Tester
COST:	$80–$120
TIP:	Pressure test your vehicles every two years when you flush and refill the radiator.

1 The pressure required by your cooling system for proper function is indicated on the radiator cap.

You can check system pressure with an inexpensive tool that combines a hand pump with a pressure gauge.

2 When the engine is cold, push down and rotate the radiator cap counter-clockwise to remove it.

3 Set the end of the pressure tool onto your radiator filler neck and rotate it clockwise to secure it. Now pump the tool until the pressure is 4 to 5 psi higher than your system's required pressure shown on your radiator cap.

4 As the pressure equalizes in the system, the reading will drop. If it stabilizes at your system's required pressure, there is no leak in your cooling system. A drop of more than a pound or two over the next 10–15 minutes indicates a leak in the system.

Chapter 6
Drivetrain

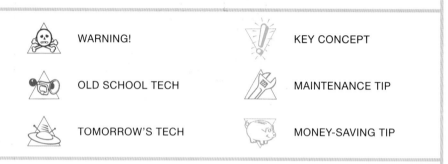

☠ WARNING!	⚠ KEY CONCEPT
OLD SCHOOL TECH	🔧 MAINTENANCE TIP
TOMORROW'S TECH	🐷 MONEY-SAVING TIP

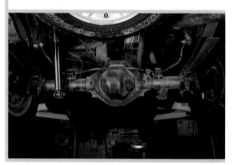

For most car owners, the key component in the drivetrain that we worry about the most is the automatic transmission— a four-, five-, or six-speed electronically controlled engineering marvel. It's the device that connects the engine to the wheels, making the car go. Working properly, it delivers incredibly smooth, fluid, seamless shifts from gear to gear. If it fails and the car won't go, you're facing a very expensive repair bill.

Your drivetrain transfers power from the car's engine to the drive wheels. A number of components are involved in doing this job. The transmission features several gear ratios—the difference between engine speed and vehicle speed—to keep the engine in its efficient power band over the vehicle's entire range of useable speeds. From the transmission, power is transferred to the drive wheels via axles and driveshafts. A differential allows the left and right drive wheels to rotate at different speeds (which is necessary for turning corners), and components like wheel bearings and universal joints keep the moving parts working smoothly.

In terms of maintenance, keep it simple. Change the lubricants in every drivetrain component every three years or 30,000–50,000 miles. That includes the transmission, transfer case (if it's four-wheel drive), and differentials.

TRANSMISSION

Transmissions come in two basic types—automatic and manual. Manual transmission has been around since the first motor vehicles and, as the name implies, involves a device, controlled by the owner/operator, that transmits power to the wheels. The automatic

BASIC REAR-WHEEL-DRIVE DRIVETRAIN COMPONENTS

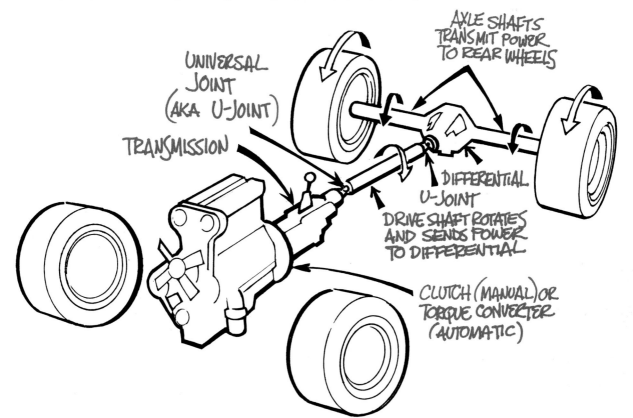

AXLE SHAFTS TRANSMIT POWER TO REAR WHEELS

UNIVERSAL JOINT (AKA U-JOINT)

TRANSMISSION

DIFFERENTIAL

U-JOINT

DRIVE SHAFT ROTATES AND SENDS POWER TO DIFFERENTIAL

CLUTCH (MANUAL) OR TORQUE CONVERTER (AUTOMATIC)

BASIC FRONT-WHEEL-DRIVE DRIVETRAIN COMPONENTS

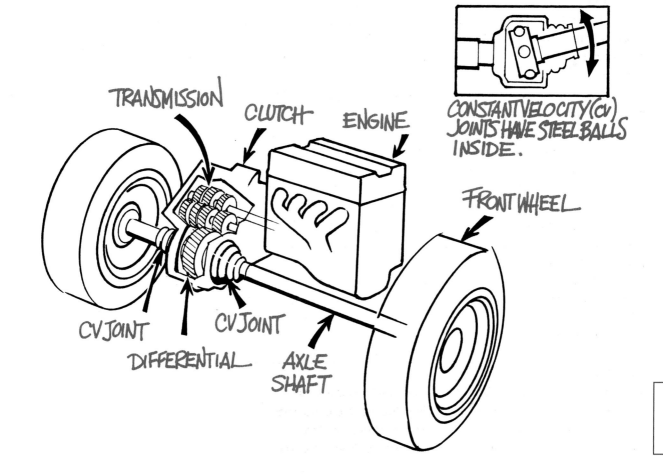

CONSTANT VELOCITY (CV) JOINTS HAVE STEEL BALLS INSIDE.

TRANSMISSION

CLUTCH

ENGINE

FRONT WHEEL

CV JOINT

CV JOINT

DIFFERENTIAL

AXLE SHAFT

transmission, on the other hand, was developed and introduced into mainstream automobiles after World War II. It requires no direct driver input once put into "drive" and leaves the operator free to focus on driving or other distractions.

But why do you need a transmission in the first place? Why not just couple the engine directly to the drive wheels—sort of like your self-propelled lawn mower? The answer, in a single word, is speed. If your lawnmower needed to be capable of 50 miles per hour, it would need a transmission. But since you can't quite walk or run that fast, the machine gets by with just one drive speed.

The primary job of any transmission is to match engine speed to vehicle speed. Internal combustion engines produce useable power over a specific range of engine speed, or rpm—revolutions per minute. This range of rpm is not broad enough to cover the range of speeds of which the vehicle is capable. More importantly, the engine has a sweet spot of rpm at which it is efficient, smooth, quiet, and powerful enough to get the job done.

So, the transmission is utilized to keep the engine in that sweet spot of rpm through the vehicle's range of speeds. At low speeds, the transmission provides a high ratio of engine speed to road speed, which delivers very good power and acceleration. As vehicle speed increases, the transmission reduces this ratio progressively, meaning the vehicle is traveling at a faster speed at the same engine rpm. There's less power available, but the vehicle is traveling at a faster speed. Ultimately, the engine will be producing its best efficiency at cruising speed, maximizing fuel mileage.

SHIFTING

How does the transmission vary the ratio of engine speed to road speed? Through gears, or speeds—as in a four-speed transmission, either manual or automatic. Each gear, or speed, provides a specific ratio of engine to road speed, starting with the highest ratio for first gear, and ending up with the lowest ratio for high gear or overdrive.

MANUAL TRANSMISSIONS

Manual transmissions feature mechanical gearsets that are engaged by the shift level operated by the driver.

MANUAL TRANSMISSION AND CLUTCH

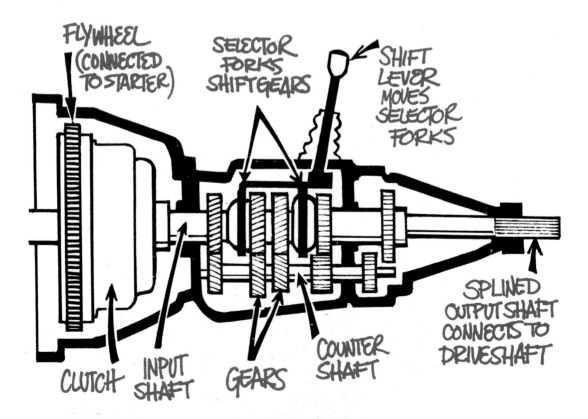

FLYWHEEL (CONNECTED TO STARTER)

SELECTOR FORKS SHIFTGEARS

SHIFT LEVER MOVES SELECTOR FORKS

SPLINED OUTPUT SHAFT CONNECTS TO DRIVESHAFT

CLUTCH   INPUT SHAFT   GEARS   COUNTER SHAFT

Automatic transmission—complete fluid and filter change at first 30,000–50,000 miles service, then complete fluid change every 30,000–50,000 miles with filter replacement every other change. It's worth noting that some carmakers no longer recommend routine fluid changes, and some don't suggest fluid changes until 100,000 miles. But virtually every transmission service professional recommends fluid service at least as often as described above.

Differential—change gear oil at every transmission service.

Transfer case—change lubricant at every transmission service.

Universal joints on driveshaft—grease at every other chassis lube if fitted with zerk, or grease fittings.

CV joints—visually inspect for torn rubber boots/contamination at every oil change.

Hubs/wheel bearings—sealed hubs, as found on many modern vehicles, require no maintenance. Conventional coaster hubs with tapered roller bearings should be checked for excessive play at every oil change. Repack bearings and replace seals every 50,000 miles. ■

MANUAL TRANSMISSION TROUBLESHOOTING

PROBLEM	PROBABLE CAUSES	ACTION TO REPAIR
INTERNAL WHINE WITH CLUTCH ENGAGED	Worn bearing inside transmission	Take to professional mechanic
WHIR FROM CLUTCH WITH FOOT ON PEDAL	Worn clutch throw-out or release bearing	Replace clutch assembly/throw-out bearing
CLUTCH SLIPPAGE/SHUDDER	Worn clutch components, bent/broken diaphragm fingers	Take to shop for diagnosis
	Broken clutch disc buffer spring; oil contamination of clutch disc	Replace clutch assembly and throw-out bearing if necessary
HEAVY/STIFF CLUTCH PEDAL	Binding clutch cable/pulley	Lubricate cable if problem persists, replace the cable
	Worn clutch pressure plate diaphragm fingers	If cable is not the problem, take to shop for diagnosis and possible replacement of the clutch assembly and throw-out bearing
SOFT/FLOPPY CLUTCH PEDAL	Damaged or broken clutch pressure plate	Take to shop for diagnosis replace clutch assembly and throw-out bearing if necessary
LOW CLUTCH PEDAL	Damaged clutch release cable	Replace clutch release cable
NO OR INCOMPLETE CLUTCH DISENGAGEMENT	Air trapped in hydraulic clutch slave/master cylinder	Check fluid level in clutch master cylinder reservoir
		Bleed clutch/replace clutch slave and master cylinder
NOISY, GRINDING, OR STIFF GEARSHIFTS	Incomplete clutch disengagement; excessive stress/worn transmission syncro assemblies	Take to shop for diagnosis; transmission repair will be needed if syncro assemblies are worn

AUTOMATIC TRANSMISSION TROUBLESHOOTING

PROBLEM	PROBABLE CAUSES	ACTION TO REPAIR
CANNOT SHIFT FROM PARK INTO GEAR	Brake/shift interlock not working	Try key on with engine not running, depress brake, shift into neutral
STARTER WILL NOT ENGAGE	Park neutral interlock problem	While trying to start, move shift lever through full range in Park then try same thing in Neutral
AUTOMATIC TRANSMISSION WILL NOT ENGAGE ANY GEAR	Low hydraulic pressure	Check fluid level and fill if necessary. *(Project 35: Check Automatic Transmission Fluid)*
	Shift lever or cable problem or misadjustment	On FWD, look for shift cable attachment point on transmission under hood. Cable may be broken/loose/disconnected
	Broken shift mechanism or cable	Adjust or replace shift mechanicsm or cable
	Hydraulic failure in transmission	Take car into a professional for diagnosis and repair
	Electronic control unit failure	Take car into a professional for diagnosis and repair
TRANSMISSION SLOW TO ENGAGE FROM PARK	Low fluid level, low hydraulic pressure	Check transmission fluid level and add as necessary. *(Project 35: Check Automatic Transmission Fluid)*
	Contaminated transmission fluid	Change transmission fluid and filter. *(Project 36: Change Transmission Fluid and Filter)*
	Worn hydraulic seals in transmission	Replace seals
SLOW OR SLUGGISH GEARSHIFTS	Low hydraulic pressure	Have professional inspect/test transmission
ENGINE REVS BUT CAR DOES NOT ACCELERATE	Transmission is slippnig	Have car towed to professional mechanic. ☠ Do not continue to drive with transmission slippage as major transmission damage can occur
TRANSMISSION SLIPS INTO NEUTRAL AT STOPS	Low hydraulic pressure	Have professional inspect/test transmission
HARD/HARSH GEARSHIFTS	Transmission in "limp" mode, meaning something in the transmission has malfunctioned and the unit is functioning on a limited mode designed to allow the car to be driven to the nearest transmission repair shop	Take car into a professional for diagnosis and repair

AUTOMATIC TRANSMISSION TROUBLESHOOTING

PROBLEM	PROBABLE CAUSES	ACTION TO REPAIR
TRANSMISSION IS STUCK IN 2ND GEAR	High hydraulic pressure	Check transmission fluid level if it is at factory recommended level, take car into a professional for diagnosis and repair. *(Project 35: Check Automatic Transmission Fluid)*
NO OVERDRIVE	Engine not fully warmed up	Have professional check and diagnose transmission
CHECK ENGINE LIGHT GOES ON	Transmission fluid overheated	Idle in park to cool fluid
	Throttle position sensor/speed sensor failure	Use 'scan' tool to diagnose transmission fault codes
RAPID, EARLY UPSHIFTS	Damaged, broken throttle valve cable in non-electronically controlled automatic transmission	Check/adjust/replace TV cable. Have professional replace/adjust cable
DELAYED HIGH-RPM UPSHIFTS	Damaged, stuck governor in non-electronically controlled automatic transmission	Add can of trasmission fluid conditioner. Have professional repair/replace internal governor
SHUDDER/VIBRATION UNDER LIGHT THROTTLE AT ROAD SPEED	Torque converter clutch slippage	Try depressing brake pedal 2 inches while maintaining speed. If shudder stops until brake is released, torque converter clutch is slipping **Fixes for slipping torque converter clutch:** Add transmission fluid additive. Confirm correct transmission fluid in unit. Change transmission fluid and filter. Replace worn torque converter *(Project 36: Change Transmission Fluid and Filter)*
TRANSMISSION FLUID LEAKING	Loose transmission line connection	Check transmission cooler lines and cooler at front of car. Tighten connections or replace lines as necessary
	Bad transmission pan gasket	Check transmission pan gasket for signs of leaking; if leaks are found, replace the gasket
	Transmission main seal (between engine and transmission) is leaking	Check for possible transmission front seal leak. If leak only leaves small stain of fluid on the transmission or a few drips on the garage floor, you can live with this until it worsens. If it leaves lots of fluid on the garage floor, the seal will need to be replaced by a professional

AUTOMATIC TRANSMISSION TROUBLESHOOTING

PROBLEM	PROBABLE CAUSES	ACTION TO REPAIR
NO FOUR-WHEEL-DRIVE ENGAGEMENT	Mechanical/vacuum/hydraulic problem with transfer case, electronic problem with transmission control unit	Check mechanical/vacuum components/connections at shift control/transfer case. Take to professional mechanic for diagnosis and repair
FOUR-WHEEL-DRIVE TRANSFER CASE WON'T SHIFT BETWEEN HIGH AND LOW RANGE	Transfer case problem	Check vacuum operation of transfer case engagement; check transfer case shift linkage check solenoid engagement of front drive axle
GRINDING/RATCHETING NOISE FROM FRONT HUB	Automatic front hub not disengaging (four-wheel-drive or front-wheel-drive vehicles only)	Overhaul or replace automatic front hubs
CLICKING NOISE FROM FRONT DRIVE AXLE ON ACCELERATION OR TURNING	Worn front drive axle shaft or CV joint	Check for torn rubber boot Replace CV joint or axle assembly
GROWL FROM FRONT HUB, VARIES WITH STEERING INPUT	Worn front wheel bearing assembly	Check wheel bearings for play or vibration in spring Replace hub and bearing assembly
HOWL FROM FRONT OR REAR DIFFERENTIAL	Low lubricant level, worn ring/pinion gears	Drain and inspect gear oil for debris/water (fill up with fresh fluid afterward) (Project 34: Change Manual Transmission Oil) Take differential cover off and inspect ring/pinion gears for wear. If worn, replace gears Check pinion bearing for play Fill differential with synthetic gear oil or add special additive
RACHETING NOISE FROM DIFFERENTIAL WHEN TURNING	Worn/binding limited-slip assembly in differential	Try adding special additive for limited slips
HEAVY HIGH-SPEED BUZZ OR VIBRATION FROM DRIVELINE WHEN ACCELERATING	Worn U-joint on driveshaft	Check for play. Replace U-joint or driveshaft if play is excessive Inspect for red oxide dust around joint. Replace U-joint or driveshaft
CLUNK JUST AS CAR COMES TO A STOP OR STARTS TO MOVE FORWARD	Bind in sliding splines on slip yoke at back of transmission	Lubricate with molybdemum disulfide grease. Remove driveshaft. Mark orientation of each end to U-joint/flange. Slide slip yoke off transmission output shaft. Clean splines and apply lubricant

Project 31
Check Differential Oil

TALENT: 2

TIME: 15 minutes

TOOLS: Screwdriver or wrench

COST: $0

TIP: Observe with vehicle sitting level.

1 The differential is in the rear axle housing of a rear-wheel-drive vehicle and front housing on four-wheel-drive vehicles.

2 To check the oil level, remove the plug located on the side of the housing or on the differential cover. This may thread in or may be a rubber plug that you can pry out with a screwdriver.

3 The oil should come up to the very bottom of the hole so that you can see or touch it through the hole. A little oil dribbles out of this differential, which is filled to the correct level.

Project 32

Change Differential Oil

TALENT:	4
TIME:	60 minutes
TOOLS:	Socket wrench, gasket scraper, cleaner, screwdriver, hammer, gasket material, or gasket
COST:	$20–$40
TIP:	A simple way to lengthen your differential's life span.

1 Loosen the bolts around the differential cover.

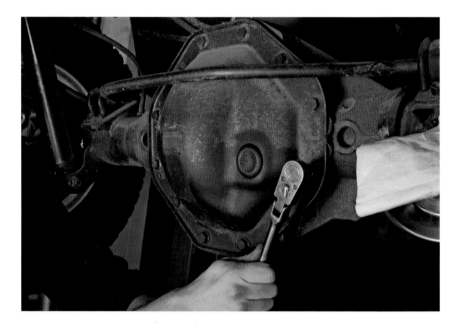

2 Sometimes paint or undercoating will gum up the bolt heads, making them hard to fit a wrench on. In that event, you can use a soft tap with a hammer to seat the wrench or socket. Be sure you have the right size socket.

Project 34
Change Manual Transmission Oil

TALENT: 2

TIME: 30–45 minutes

TOOLS: Wrench, drain pain, flexible hose

COST: $10–$15

TIP: Fill level is usually to bottom of fill hole.

1 Remove the drain plug with an appropriate pan placed below it to catch the oil. If there's no drain plug, leave this task to a pro.

2 After allowing the oil to drain for a few minutes, put the drain plug back in. Tighten securely.

3 Add the correct oil. Older designs used heavier gear oils, but most of today's manual transmissions are filled with automatic transmission fluid. Your owner's manual will tell you the correct quantity and type to purchase, along with the service interval. The typical fill level is to the bottom of the fill hole. A short length of hose fitted to the oil spout, or an inexpensive pump attachment for the oil bottle, may ease filling.

Project 35
Check Transmission Fluid

TALENT:	1
TIME:	5 minutes
TOOLS:	Dipstick
COST:	$0
TIP:	Vehicles don't burn transmission fluid; if it's low, you have a leak that should be fixed.

1 Check the transmission fluid with the engine fully warmed up and running. The transmission fluid dipstick will be in the engine bay and may be labeled with words or a symbol. Your owner's manual will identify its location, markings, and the transmission's fluid capacity.

2 Pull the dipstick and wipe it clean with a cloth or paper towel.

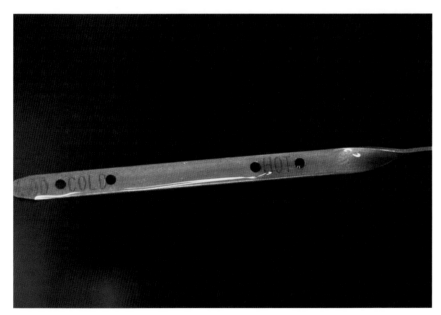

3 With the engine warm, the fluid should reach the "full/hot" mark on the dipstick. This late model Dodge Dakota has the appropriate fluid level.

Project 36
Change Automatic Transmission Fluid and Filter
(Front-Wheel Drive/Rear-Wheel Drive)

TALENT:	5
TIME:	1-2 hours
TOOLS:	Socket wrench, extender, cleaner, gasket scraper/remover, hammer, screwdriver, gasket material, or gasket
COST:	$15–$50
TIP:	Your transmission may have two filters; replace both at once, or as recommended by manufacturer.

1 The automatic transmission pan is on the underside of the transmission, which is bolted to the engine. The top photo shows a rear-wheel-drive vehicle (side view). The lower photo shows a front-wheel-drive (front view). We've used a lift here for photography, but this operation can easily be performed with the car safely up on jack stands. (See How To Jack Up Your Car in Chapter 1.)

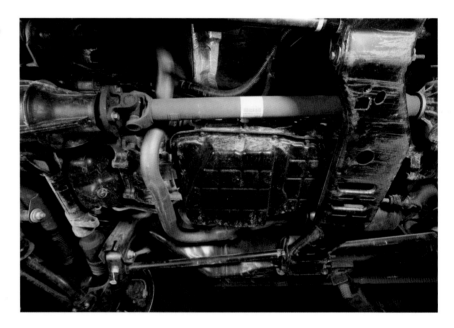

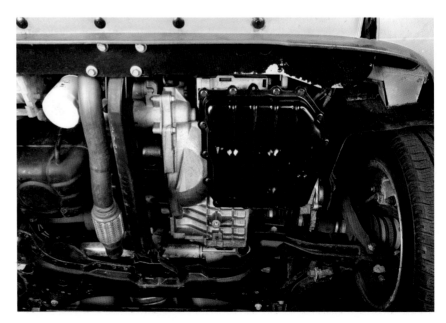

2 Remove the bolts on the transmission pan with an appropriate ratchet or air wrench. By loosening and lowering one end first, most of the fluid will drain from one spot, making it easier to catch it in the drain pan.

3 Leave two bolts loosened but still threaded in on roughly opposite sides of the pan. That way, when you pry it free, it won't drop down and make a huge mess.

4 Many transmissions have two filters, one for the transmission itself (1) and the other for the transmission oil cooler (2).

1

2

5 The transmission filter may be removed with a screwdriver, wrench, or torx (star) wrench.

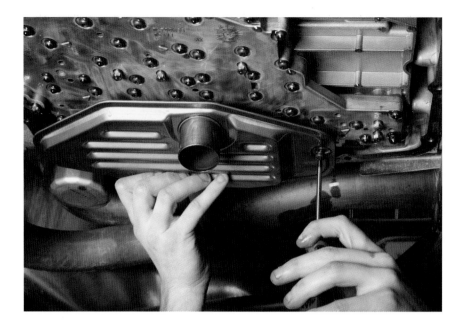

6 The transmission cooler filter may require a small oil-filter wrench.

7 Scrape the old gasket from the pan with a gasket scraper or razor blade as needed, and polish the mating surface with Scotch-Brite. Then clean and flush the pan thoroughly with a strong cleaner, such as brake cleaner.

 Never push a tool toward your other hand. Also wear rubber gloves any time you clean a part with a strong cleaner or solvent.

8 Many transmission pans seal with a liquid-style gasket that is spread along the contact surface. Your dealer or auto parts store will tell you what you need. Wetting your finger will keep the sealer from sticking to it as you spread it in a thin, even coating across the whole contact area. Install the new filters and reinstall the pan, snugging the bolts in a crisscross pattern.

9 Automatic transmissions are usually filled through the dipstick hole.

10 Use a funnel and the correct quantity and type of fluid recommended in your owner's manual. Check level with transmission dipstick as in Project 35, Check Automatic Transmission Fluid.

Chapter 7
Suspension and Steering

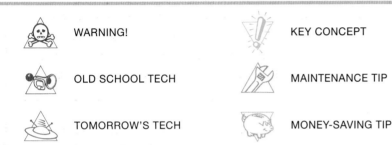

WARNING!	KEY CONCEPT
OLD SCHOOL TECH	MAINTENANCE TIP
TOMORROW'S TECH	MONEY-SAVING TIP

THE SHOCK ABSORBER

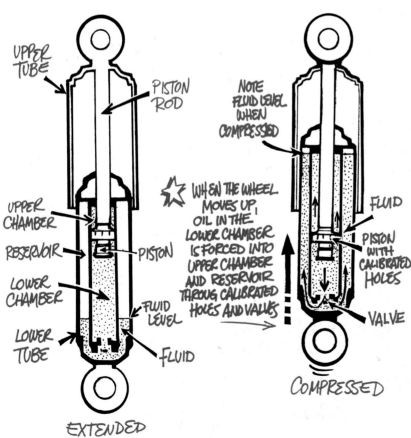

UPPER TUBE

PISTON ROD

NOTE FLUID LEVEL WHEN COMPRESSED

UPPER CHAMBER

RESERVOIR

PISTON

LOWER CHAMBER

FLUID LEVEL

★ WHEN THE WHEEL MOVES UP, OIL IN THE LOWER CHAMBER IS FORCED INTO UPPER CHAMBER AND RESERVOIR THROUGH CALIBRATED HOLES AND VALVES

FLUID

PISTON WITH CALIBRATED HOLES

LOWER TUBE

FLUID

VALVE

EXTENDED

COMPRESSED

From the very earliest days of the automobile, carmakers have incorporated steering and suspension systems into their vehicles for two very important reasons. Keep the tires planted firmly on the pavement so that they can develop the traction or grip necessary to steer, stop and accelerate the vehicle. Secondly, do this job smoothly and comfortably so that you don't spend half your time at the chiropractor and the other half at the dentist having your filings redone. Today's vehicles are far more sophisticated, and their suspension and steering

SUSPENSION/STEERING TROUBLESHOOTING

PROBLEM	PROBABLE CAUSES	ACTION TO REPAIR
LOUD WHINE WHEN STEERING IS TURNED	Low power steering fluid	Check fluid level in power steering reservoir Fill with correct fluid if necessary. (See owner's manual for fluid type and instructions on level) *(Project 37: Check Power Steering Fluid)*
	Worn power steering pump	Replace power steering pump
REDDISH FLUID PUDDLES UNDER CAR	Power steering fluid leak	Check hoses/connections; tighten if possible
		Replace leaking hose
		Front seal leak on power steering pump; replace seal or replace pump
SUSPENSION RATTLES OR CLUNKS	Loose shock absorber	Tighten mounting bolts
	Worn shock and/or strut bushings	Replace shock and strut bushings
	Worn, damaged, or failed shock absorber or strut cartridge	Have replacement shocks or struts installed at repair shop
	Worn or broken sway bar link	Have link replaced at repair shop
	Worn control arm bushing	Have bushing replaced at repair shop
	Broken coil spring	Have coil spring replaced at repair shop
	Worn strut upper bearing plate	Have shop replace bearing plate
UNEVEN RIDE HEIGHT	Damaged or broken spring or torsion bar	Take to shop and have spring replaced and/or the torsion bar adjusted
	Damaged air suspension system/ component	Have system checked by professional
POOR RIDE QUALITY	Improperly inflated tires	Check tire pressure and inflate all four tires to carmaker's recommended psi
	Worn or damaged shocks or struts	Have replacement shocks or struts installed at repair shop
	Worn/damaged suspension component	Have suspension inspected at repair shop
CAR BOUNCES UP AND DOWN/STEERING WHEEL SHAKES AFTER CROSSING BUMPS	Worn shocks/struts	Have shocks/struts replaced at repair shop

Project 37

Check Power Steering Fluid

TALENT:	1
TIME:	5 minutes
TOOLS:	Dipstick
COST:	$0
TIP:	Dipstick may be marked for hot and cold check levels—use appropriate mark.

1 The power steering fluid reservoir is usually clearly marked. It should be near the front of your engine, or opposite the transmission, where the power-steering pump is driven by a pulley.

2 With the engine off and relatively cool, turn the cap counterclockwise and remove.

3 This dipstick shows the level cold. Some power-steering dipsticks have markings for cold and hot. If the level is low, top up the system with the proper power-steering fluid. Check your owner's manual for the specific fluid recommendations.

TIP: Vehicles don't consume power steering fluid. If yours is low, check for signs of leaks in the system and on the ground.

Project 38

Lubricate Steering Linkage

TALENT: 2

TIME: 30 minutes

TOOLS: Grease gun

COST: Less than a dollar in grease

TIP: Don't overfill fittings.

1 The steering linkage on many vehicles (but not all) incorporates grease fittings, called zerk fittings, that allow you to lube linkage joints.

2 Click coupler on the end of the grease gun's hose over each fitting and pump carefully until you see the rubber boot start to bulge, then stop. Generally three or four pumps will do the job. Don't over lube the fitting—you might rupture the rubber boot. Wipe off all excess grease with a shop rag or paper towel.

Chapter 8
Tires and Wheels

WARNING!

OLD SCHOOL TECH

TOMORROW'S TECH

KEY CONCEPT

MAINTENANCE TIP

MONEY-SAVING TIP

Quick, what are the most important components on your automobile? Before answering, think about how your motor vehicle works. When you want it to go, what do you do? Push the throttle, right? And to stop, you push the brake pedal, right? And to negotiate a corner, you turn the steering wheel. As the driver, all you're doing is pushing a couple of pedals and turning a wheel. The vehicle must translate your wishes to "go, stop, steer" into a force on the pavement that actually accelerates, slows, or turns the vehicle.

And your vehicle does this through its tires—those simple, black round rubber donuts mounted on each wheel. What irony, the relatively lowest cost components on the vehicle are by far the most critical to its operation and performance—and your safety. That's precisely why you need to pay full and complete attention to your tires.

In the world of tires, some things change and some things stay the same. Just like the earliest pneumatic tires, today's tires are still made from rubber, fabrics, and steel and are inflated with air. Today's tires feature extremely sophisticated technology and space-age materials that allow them to develop much higher levels of performance and last tens of thousands of miles longer than their turn-of-the-century counterparts.

Today's tires can perform well in a wide variety of road conditions—dry, wet, mud, snow, and ice—while providing a smooth, quiet ride, resisting punctures from nails, screws, and road debris, and delivering 50,000–75,000 or more miles of service. And all this for somewhere between $50 and $150 for a typical all-season passenger car tire. If you're looking for the automotive bargain of all time, you found it: tires!

TIRE SHOPPING 101

So, when you're shopping for new tires, what are your primary concerns? Price? Warranty? Tread life? All these are important, obviously, but don't forget to focus on the tire's primary job, gripping the pavement to provide traction for your vehicle to go, stop, and steer. The key issues in grip—a nice visual image of how a tire develops traction—are sidewall construction, rubber compound, and tread design. That's why you'll find tires of the same size offered as all-season, highway, winter, snow, and performance designs. Each features a particular combination of design and material specifications to maximize that particular characteristic of the tire's performance.

Simple examples illustrate this.

Performance tires typically feature a softer rubber in the tread compound for better grip, a shorter sidewall (lower aspect ratio/profile) for quicker steering response and less sidewall flex, and a tread design that maximizes the amount of rubber on the pavement.

TREAD COMPARISONS

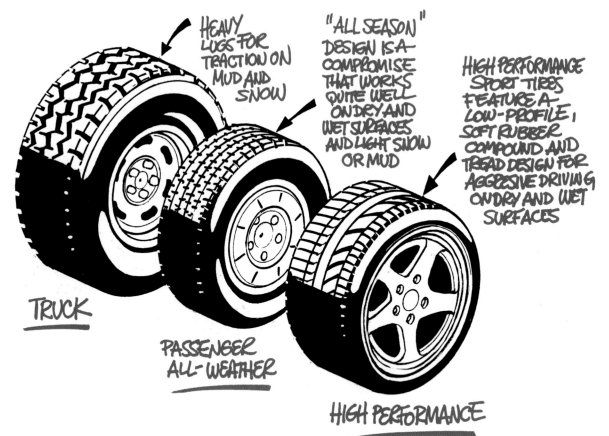

HEAVY LUGS FOR TRACTION ON MUD AND SNOW

"ALL SEASON" DESIGN IS A COMPROMISE THAT WORKS QUITE WELL ON DRY AND WET SURFACES AND LIGHT SNOW OR MUD

HIGH PERFORMANCE SPORT TIRES FEATURE A LOW-PROFILE, SOFT RUBBER COMPOUND AND TREAD DESIGN FOR AGGRESSIVE DRIVING ON DRY AND WET SURFACES

TRUCK

PASSENGER ALL-WEATHER

HIGH PERFORMANCE

Snow tires, on the other hand, feature deep tread lugs and wide tread grooves to move snow out from under the tread, and a relatively narrow design to cut through, rather than ride on top of, the snow.

All-season tires have a compromise design that feature many sipes, or fine slits or grooves, in the tread surface to pump or channel water out from under the tire, coupled with a quiet, long-life design that delivers tens of thousands of miles of service in any conditions.

ASSESSING TIRE WEAR

Remember the absolute key to automotive tires: how well the tread surface on the tire grips the pavement. The tire can only do this if it is in good condition, properly inflated, and not worn abnormally—or worn out completely! The deeper the tread surface (new passenger car tires typically come with about 10/32 inch of tread), the better the tire can grip the pavement in wet conditions. Literally, the grooves in the tread surface are a water pump that can be rated in gallons per hour. As the tire wears and the tread grooves become shallower, the efficiency of the pumping action deteriorates. That means a tire with only 3/32 inch of tread won't be anywhere near as effective in main-taining traction in wet, slippery conditions as the same

tire with as-new tread depth. The message here is don't wait until the mandated tread-wear indicators begin to show at roughly 2/32–3/32 inch of remaining tread. Replace the tires on your vehicle when tread depth drops below roughly 4/32–5/32 inch of tread. Simple reason: better safe than sorry.

TIRE PRESSURE

The other key factor in tire performance is inflation pressure. Check the door post, glove box, or owner's manual for the carmaker's recommendations for tire pressure; these are the correct tire inflation pressures for your vehicle. For passenger cars, inflation pres-sures will typically be in the 28–40-psi range; for light trucks, a 35–50-psi range. Note that each tire will also carry a maximum pressure for maximum load rating, but the correct tire pressures for your vehicle are those recommended by the carmaker.

But let's simplify this. For any motor vehicle (car or truck), never let tire pressures drop below approxi-mately 30 psi while cold. At 30 psi or above, the tire sidewall will be stable and responsive to quick steering inputs, the tread surface will maintain full contact with the pavement, operating temperatures will remain stable and safe, and the tire will develop maximum

UNDERSTANDING THE NUMBERS

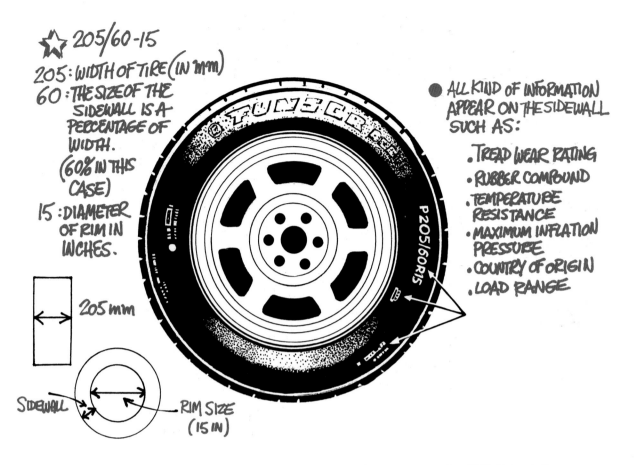

☆ 205/60-15

205: WIDTH OF TIRE (IN mm)
60: THE SIZE OF THE SIDEWALL IS A PERCENTAGE OF WIDTH. (60% IN THIS CASE)
15: DIAMETER OF RIM IN INCHES.

205 mm

SIDEWALL

RIM SIZE (15 IN)

● ALL KIND OF INFORMATION APPEAR ON THE SIDEWALL SUCH AS:
- TREAD WEAR RATING
- RUBBER COMPOUND
- TEMPERATURE RESISTANCE
- MAXIMUM INFLATION PRESSURE
- COUNTRY OF ORIGIN
- LOAD RANGE

traction and deliver maximum mileage. This is a solid rule-of-thumb to follow, but again, check the exact pressure recommendations from the carmaker.

Oh yeah, maintain these pressures by checking your tire pressures at least once per month. Tires have a funny habit of losing pressure slowly. Air can escape through the microscopic porosity of the tire itself—or the not-so-microscopic nail hole! Air can also leak from the rim/bead area—where the tire meets and seats to the rim—and through the porosity of the rim itself, particularly with aluminum and alloy wheels. And finally, tire pressure will drop simply due to changes in outside air temperature. In fall and winter, tire pressures will drop roughly 1 pound per 10-degree drop in air temperature. That means a tire with slightly low air pressure, perhaps 25 psi in August, might have less than 20 psi in January—a prime candidate for a flat tire at a most inconvenient time and place, after work in a dark, freezing parking lot!

TIRES BY THE NUMBERS

When you buy a new set of tires, the invoice shows the make, model, and size of the tire. Size is indicated by that strange looking P-metric description. For example: P205/60R15 89H or LT265/75R16 C.

P	Passenger car tire; LT light truck tire
205	Section width in millimeters—the actual width of the tire from inner sidewall bulge to outer sidewall bulge
60	Aspect ratio—the ratio of the tire's sidewall height to its section width, 60 defines a tire with a sidewall height 60 percent of its section width
R	Radial construction—means the tire is built with its structural cords or belts laid across the shortest distance from bead to bead, exactly perpendicular to the rolling axis of the tire; radial tires perform far better and have completely replaced earlier bias-ply tires
15	The nominal rim diameter in inches
89	Load index of the tire—defines the maximum load in pounds that the tire can vertically support safely when inflated to a specific inflation pressure
C	Load range for light truck tire—defines the range of horizontal loads the tire can handle; the higher the load range, B through G, the stiffer the sidewall; particularly useful for trailers being towed
H	Speed rating of tire—defines the maximum speed for which the tire is rated; an H rating indicates a maximum speed of 130 miles per hour

BALANCING A WHEEL

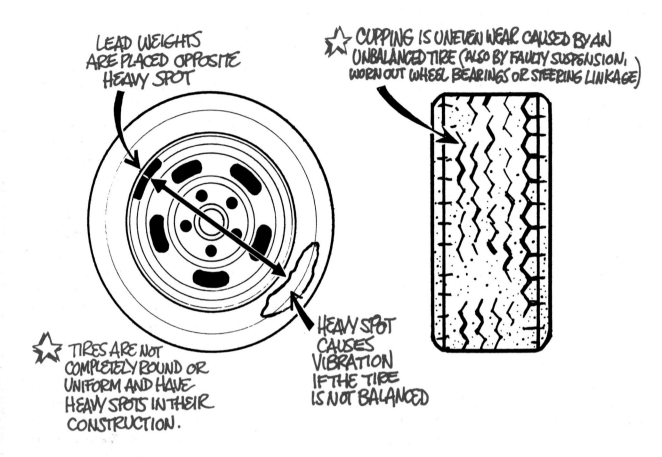

LEAD WEIGHTS ARE PLACED OPPOSITE HEAVY SPOT

☆ **CUPPING IS UNEVEN WEAR CAUSED BY AN UNBALANCED TIRE (ALSO BY FAULTY SUSPENSION, WORN OUT WHEEL BEARINGS OR STEERING LINKAGE)**

☆ **TIRES ARE NOT COMPLETELY ROUND OR UNIFORM AND HAVE HEAVY SPOTS IN THEIR CONSTRUCTION.**

HEAVY SPOT CAUSES VIBRATION IF THE TIRE IS NOT BALANCED

MORE LETTER AND NUMBERS

Today's tires carry a great deal of additional information stamped into the sidewall of the tire. In addition to the tiremaker's name and model, you'll also find information including the following on the sidewall:

Radial—as described in previous section, radial cord construction

Tubeless—as the name implies, no tube required, for the inner surface of the tire liner is vulcanized to seal it completely, eliminating the need for a tube

Tread X Plies/Sidewall X Plies—the number and rating of the layers, or plies, in the construction and tread of the tire

Max load/Max Pressure—the pressure at which the tire can support its maximum vertical load, again not necessarily the correct inflation pressure for that vehicle

DOT—U.S. Department of Transportation safety standard code

Treadwear—tiremaker's comparative rating of this tire's wear characteristics; the higher the number, the longer the tire will wear

Traction—AA, A, B, or C rating; tiremaker's rating for traction capability in combined wet and dry conditions, with AA being best and C being acceptable.

Temperature—A, B, and C rating, tiremaker's rating for tire's ability to withstand heat, with A being best

MUD AND SNOW TIRES

If you live in a climate where roads are wet, snow covered, or icy a significant part of each year, make sure the tires that you choose for your vehicle are designed to perform well in slippery conditions. The Rubber Manufacturers Association has developed a specific set of standards for mud and snow (M&S) tires. The designation M&S on the sidewall specifies a standard for the number and angle of tread grooves to help ensure the tire is effective at pumping water out from under the tread to maximize traction in wet, slippery conditions. If your driving routine includes these conditions, look/ask for M&S-rated tires for your passenger car or light truck.

TAKING CARE OF YOUR TIRES

Automotive tires are tough—very, very tough. We have them mounted, inflated, and bolted to our vehicles, then we forget 'em. Yet they continue to save our bacon by providing superb traction in a wide variety of conditions, mile after mile, day after day, year after year—even when we don't keep their pressures up, when we bounce them off curbs and when we pound them through potholes. Like I said, tough.

But not bulletproof. Tires still go flat from screws, nails, road debris, and owner neglect. Flat tires still fail; just look at the chunks of tire and rubber debris along the side of any road or highway. And tire failures still contribute to crashes, injuries, and fatalities.

So . . . take care of your tires. As mentioned earlier, check tire pressures once a month, or more often if you identify a problem tire with a slow leak. A $10 digital tire-pressure gauge in the glove box is a simple, inexpensive investment in the latest state-of-the-art equipment for measuring tire pressure. Check your tire pressures cold (before driving the vehicle) in order to have a consistent baseline for comparison.

Don't forget to check the spare tire periodically. Wouldn't want to find it flat just when you need it, would you? And here's a hint: carry a can or two of aerosol tire inflator in your trunk. This doesn't permanently fix a flat tire and, if the tire is significantly damaged or torn, this product won't help. But if the slow leak finally left the wrong tire flat in the wrong neighborhood in the wrong weather, injecting a can of tire inflator might inflate the tire enough to allow you to drive to a safe location or the tire shop.

Remember, if you use products like these, you must have the tire repaired or replaced as soon as possible. Don't forget to tell the tire shop or technician so that he/she can safely remove the inflating gas and sealing material before attempting to repair the tire.

Any tire that loses more than a couple of pounds of pressure per month should be checked by a professional. Bead leaks around the rim—particularly common with the second and third sets of tires mounted on a rim—can be corrected by breaking the tire bead from the rim, then cleaning and polishing the bead area to remove corrosion and debris and applying a special sealer to help prevent future leaks.

Visual Inspection

Obviously, if a tire is losing air, look and feel for punctures. Visually inspect the entire tread surface for the nail or screw head staring at you. If the tire is still

inflated, you probably don't want to pull the nail/screw out or you'll have the opportunity to actually watch the tire go flat right before your eyes.

Keep an eye out for any deep cuts in the tread surface, or cuts/splits in the sidewall that might indicate a serious or structural problem with the tire. And finally, put on a pair of light work or garden gloves and gently sweep your hands over the entire tread surface of the tire. Any bumps, lumps, or irregularities indicate a potential belt separation internally, physical damage to the carcass, or uneven wear pattern from a suspension or steering problem.

While you're at it, check the remaining tread depth on each tire. A small inexpensive tire tread depth gauge costs just a few dollars, but if you left your gold-plated gauge at home, just use a penny. Insert the coin, with the President's head down, into the deepest tread groove you can find. If the top of his head shows above the tread, it's time to replace the tire.

Is it worth all this effort just for a $75 tire? How much is your vehicle, your life, and your family worth? Keeping your tires properly inflated and identifying and correcting the start of an unusual wear pattern will maximize the tire's life expectancy and mileage. Add frequent tire rotation to equalize tire wear between all four tires, and you'll get your money's worth from each tire on your vehicle.

Speaking of tire rotation patterns, cross-rotation patterns are back in. For rear-wheel- and all-wheel-drive vehicles, rotate the front tires to the opposite rear corner, and move the rear tires straight forward to the front. For front-wheel-drive vehicles, swap the rear tires onto the opposite front corners, and move the front tires to the rear on the same side. Rotate your tires every 6,000–8,000 miles, which conveniently falls at every other oil change.

Please note that many of today's performance tires are directional, meaning they are designed to rotate only in one direction. Unless you dismount the tire from the rim, flip it over, and remount it, the only rotation you can do is to swap the tires front to back on the same side.

And there are a few vehicles that have proprietary tires on each corner—newer Corvettes come to mind. The tires are not only directional, but different sizes front to back. No tire rotation is possible, or necessary, with these vehicles.

TIRE REPLACEMENT

If you've rotated your tires regularly, kept them properly inflated, and managed to avoid hitting too many curbs

WHEEL BEARING BASICS

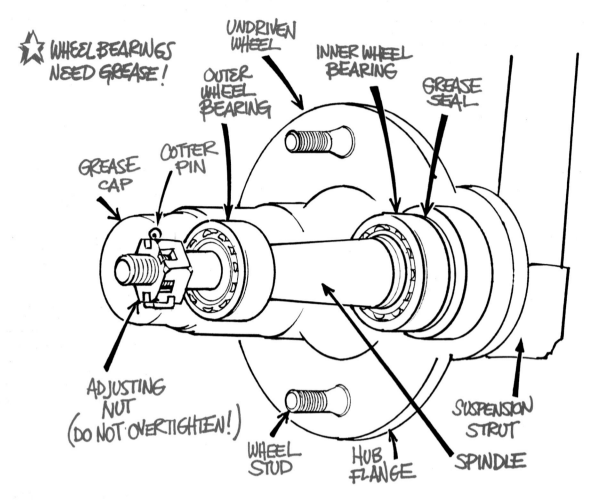

☆ WHEEL BEARINGS NEED GREASE!

UNDRIVEN WHEEL

INNER WHEEL BEARING

OUTER WHEEL BEARING

GREASE SEAL

GREASE CAP

COTTER PIN

ADJUSTING NUT (DO NOT OVERTIGHTEN!)

WHEEL STUD

HUB FLANGE

SPINDLE

SUSPENSION STRUT

and potholes, you'll be able to replace the entire set of tires at one time, and that's always the best policy. Installing a complete new set of tires means you'll continue to have a matched set of the proper make, model, and size tire on your vehicle.

But what if you didn't rotate your tires regularly, and the front pair or rear pair wears out first? Or a huge pothole won its bout with one of your tires? Or you didn't bother to check the alignment and one of the front tires is worn dramatically. Can you replace just one tire? Or just a pair?

Certainly, but make absolutely sure you find a matching tire or tires to install on your vehicle. Even though the tire may carry the same size designation, unless it is a direct replacement, or better yet, the exact make, model, and size, you may end up with mismatched tires on your vehicle.

A complete set of matched tires is of critical importance on four-wheel- and all-wheel-drive vehicles. The drivetrains on vehicles do not deal well

with tires of different sizes or diameters, even when that difference is very small. Significant driveline damage to differentials can occur if the two tires on the vehicle are of different sizes, or even worn so that the difference in rolling diameter is more than a few 10ths of an inch.

If you're so inclined, you can check the diameter with a simple tape measure and a piece of chalk. Mark the sidewall of the tire and the pavement at the center of its contact patch, then roll the vehicle forward one full revolution of the tire, and mark the pavement adjacent to the chalk mark on the sidewall. Now, just measure the distance—the circumference of the tire—with the tape measure. Repeat for the other tires on your vehicle, and compare your measurements. Any significant mismatch could lead to driveline problems and premature tire wear on driven axles.

It's really simple: take care of your tires and they will take care of you and your family. ∎

TIRE AND WHEEL TROUBLESHOOTING

PROBLEM	PROBABLE CAUSES	ACTION TO REPAIR
VIBRATION OR PULSATION IN STEERING WHEEL OR CHASSIS	Low tire pressure	Check tire pressure and inflate all four tires to carmaker's recommended psi. *(Project 39: Check Tire Pressure)*
	Worn or damaged tire(s)	Inspect tires for obvious problems (bulges, flat spots, or unusual wear) *(Project 40: Assess Tire Wear)*
	Tires or wheels out of balance	Have tires rebalanced at repair shop. Note: If a standard tire balancing doesn't cure your vibration problem, find a shop with a more sophisticated "Road Force" balancer
REAR END OF VEHICLE FEELS LOOSE, UNSTABLE	Very low or flat rear tire.	Pull over carefully and check tire. If it is flat, replace with spare. NOTE: Have tire inspected/repaired by tire shop. *(Project 41: Change Tire)*
	Tire or wheel is out of round	Visually inspect rim and tire for obvious problems. If none visible, take to tire repair shop and have wheel checked for damage, run-out (tire/wheel is like warped phonograph record generates a wobble while rolling down road) and out-of-round (tire/wheel is egg-shaped generates a pulsing motion while rolling down road)
BRAKE VIBRATION	See **Brake Troubleshooting**	
BULGE ON SIDEWALL AND/OR DISTORTED TREAD SURFACE	Damaged tire from impact/belt/tread separation	Have tire replaced
UNEVEN TREADWEAR ON TIRES	Tires not properly balanced	Have tires rebalanced at tire shop
	Tires/wheels not properly aligned	Have tires/wheels aligned at tire shop
TIRE WORN IN CENTER	Overinflated tire	Deflate to carmaker's recommended psi. *(Project 39: Check Tire Pressure; Project 42: Rotate Tires)*
TIRE WORN ON BOTH OUTER EDGES	Underinflated tire	Inflate to carmaker's recommended psi. *(Project 39: Check Tire Pressure; Project 42: Rotate Tires)*
TIRE WORN ON INNER OR OUTER EDGE	Alignment problem	Take to tire shop and have wheel alignment checked
TIRE CUPPED OR FEATHERED ON EDGE	Alignment/suspension problem	Take to tire shop and have wheel alignment checked
	Tires not rotated at proper intervals	
TIRE SIDEWALL DAMAGED, CUT, OR GOUGED	Damaged tire	Have tire checked by professional to determine safety. Replace if necessary
TIRE IS WEATHERCHECKED OR HAS SMALL SIDEWALL CRACKS	Aged, weatherchecked tire	Replace tire
DAMAGED OR BENT WHEEL		Replace or repair bent or damaged wheel
FLAT TIRE, SOFT TIRE, OR TIRE THAT HAS A SLOW LEAK	Small hole in tire, leaky bead, bad valve stem	Take tire to tire shop for professional repair

Project 39
Check Tire Pressure

TALENT:	1
TIME:	10 minutes
TOOLS:	Pressure gauge
COST:	Tool cost: $2–$10
TIP:	Tires lose 1 psi per month on average, so check and top up regularly for long, safe service.

1 Air pressure should be measured when the tire is cold—that is, before driving on it. Recommended inflation pressures in your manual and on the tire's sidewall apply to a cold tire. Remove valve stem cap.

2 Press the tire pressure gauge onto the valve stem so that the gauge's receptacle engages squarely.

3 The pressure within the tire will force a graded stick out the back of the gauge on this type. You can also purchase a gauge with a round dial where the psi is indicated by a needle. Your best choice is a digital tire pressure gauge.

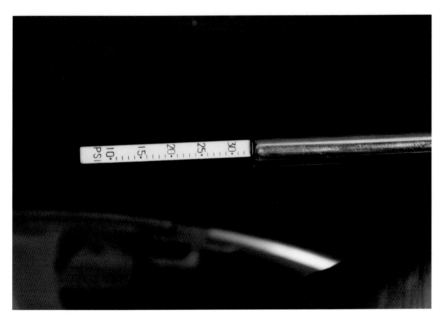

4 Remove the gauge and read it in good light.

TIP: Remember to check and inflate your spare tire, too, so that it's ready if you need it. Check tires once a month and maintain proper pressure for safe handling and long tire life.

CHECK TIRE PRESSURE

Project 40
Assess Tire Wear

TALENT: 1

TIME: 10 minutes

TOOLS: Penny or tread-depth
          gauge

COST: Tool cost: 1 cent to $8

TIP: Wear should be even over
          the tread surface. If not,
          the tire has been
          improperly inflated, or
          there is an alignment
          or suspension problem.

1 Telling a good tire from a worn one
isn't always easy by sight alone. The
tire on the right is good; the left tire is
ready to be replaced.

2 An old standby for measuring tire
wear is the penny test. Insert a penny
into the tread with Lincoln's head
pointed down and facing you. If you
can see the top of his head, the tire is
ready for replacement.

3 A new tire has considerably more tread depth. That depth provides channels through which rain, snow, and mud can escape so the tire doesn't ride up on them. When tread gets too thin, traction drops off dramatically.

4 A tread depth gauge is an inexpensive tool. This one shows depth in 1/32-inch increments. The more worn of our two tires shows only about 3/32 inch of tread depth, meaning it's due for replacement.

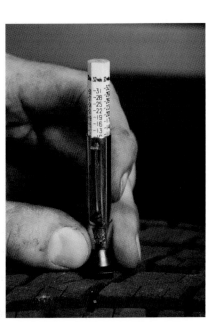

5 The good tire has about 10/32 inch.

Project 41
Change Tire

TALENT:	2
TIME:	15–45 minutes
TOOLS:	Vehicle jack, tire iron, and spare
COST:	$0
TIP:	Check your spare tire and keep it inflated along with your mounted tires, so it can serve you when you need it.

1 Everyone who drives a vehicle should know how to change a tire. It starts with knowing where the jack, lug wrench, and spare tire are stowed in the vehicle. This minivan's tools lie beneath a cover at the rear. Instructions are on the inside of the cover.

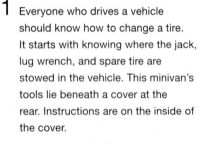

The vehicle must be on level ground to change a tire. Never jack up a vehicle on an incline because the vehicle can roll or shift when you lift the wheel(s) off the ground. Wear gloves to protect your hands.

2 With the tire on the ground, "break" the lug nuts free so they will turn easily once you raise the vehicle. If you jack up the vehicle first, the wheel will spin when you push on the tire wrench.

3 The jack is designed to fit in a particular place. On modern vehicles the jacking point is often where sheet metal comes together to form a ridge, called a pinch weld. Check the jacking instructions or owner's manual. This scissor jack rises when you turn a nut on one end.
The wrench that turns the nut is the same one used to loosen the wheel's lug nuts.

⚠ Do not work under a vehicle supported by a tire jack. It does not provide adequate lift, stability, or safety for that purpose.

4 With the lug nuts loosened, jack up the vehicle until the tire clears the ground. Take the lug nuts off, pull the wheel off, and set it aside.

TIP: If the lug nuts are too tight for you to turn, put the wrench securely on the nut with the handle pointing to the left, then press it down with your foot for better leverage.

5 The spare tire in this Dodge Caravan is suspended underneath the van's rear end. To lower it, remove a plastic cap in the floor, exposing a nut that can be turned with the jack's wrench. Place the wrench on the nut and turn counterclockwise.

CHANGE TIRE

6 This lever releases the spare tire.
Check your owner's manual for spare
tire release procedures on your car.

7 Lift the spare tire onto the wheel
studs. If it's too heavy to lift by hand,
sit on the ground in front of the wheel
opening and use your feet to help lift
the wheel into place. Thread all the
lug nuts onto the studs and hand-
tighten them with the lug wrench.
Lower the jack until the tread makes
contact with the ground, but don't
set full vehicle weight on it. This way,
the wheel won't spin when you fully
tighten the lugs using a crisscross
pattern. Double check that all the
lugs are securely tightened, lower the
vehicle, stow jack, throw the flat tire
in the back.

TIP: Fix your spare as soon as you
can, even if it's not a "mini" spare. If
you let it go, you may need a spare
again and not have one.

Project 42
Rotate Tires

TALENT: 2

TIME: 60 minutes

TOOLS: Jack, jack stands, vehicle's tire iron

COST: $0

TIP: Mark tires with chalk before removal to keep track of which one came from and goes where.

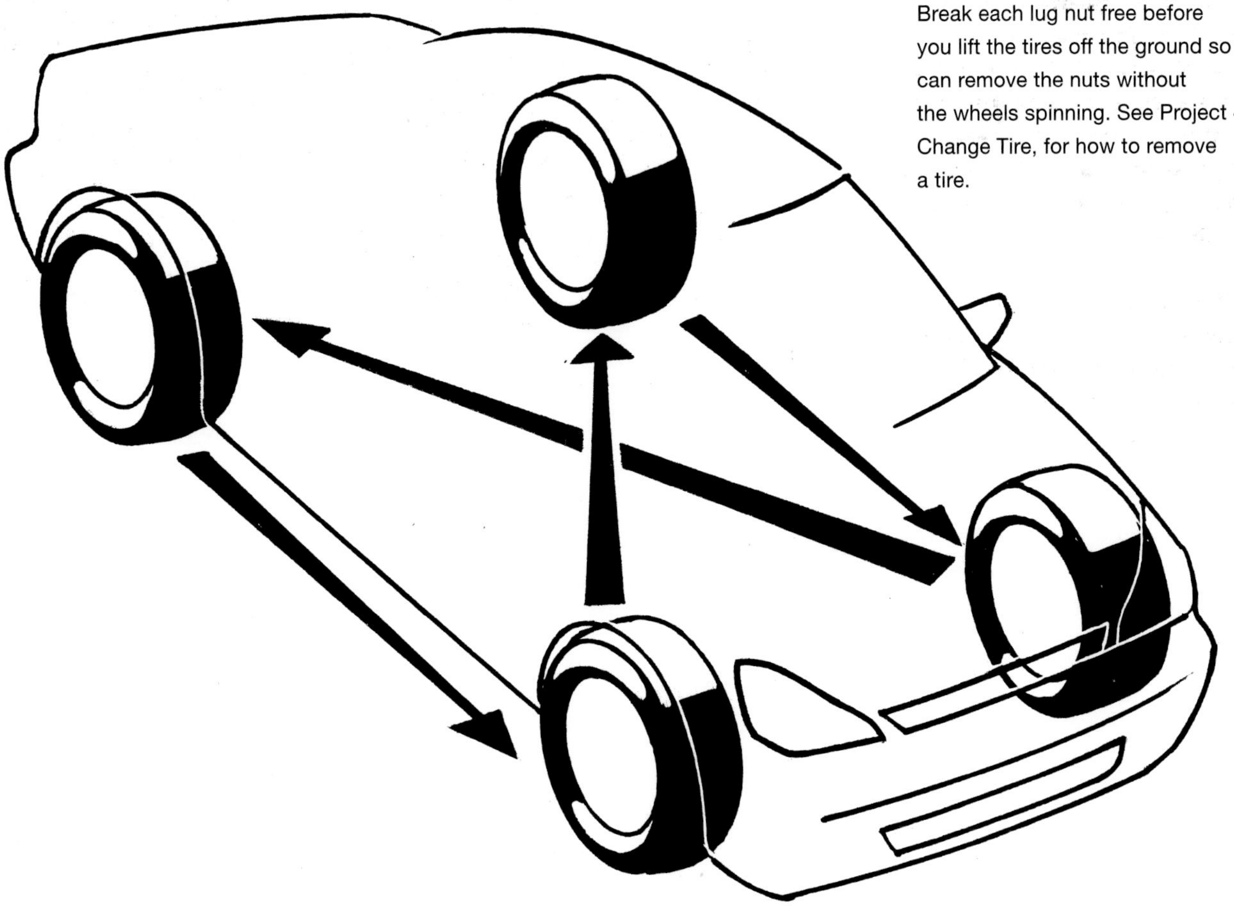

1 If your vehicle has tires and wheels of the same size in both front and back, you can rotate your own tires. The easiest way to do this is to set the car safely on jack stands. (See How To Jack Up Your Car in Chapter 1 for a description.)

Break each lug nut free before you lift the tires off the ground so you can remove the nuts without the wheels spinning. See Project 41: Change Tire, for how to remove a tire.

Chapter 9
Brakes

WARNING!

OLD SCHOOL TECH

TOMORROW'S TECH

KEY CONCEPT

MAINTENANCE TIP

MONEY-SAVING TIP

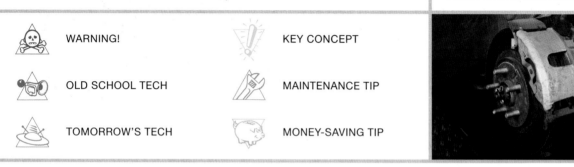

No doubt about it, the brake system on your automobile has to work properly and stop your vehicle quickly and safely every single time you need it to. How do they work? Think of the brake assemblies on each wheel as small engines. The engine under the hood converts the energy in fuel into heat by combustion, then converts that heat into mechanical work to propel the car, right?

Think of each brake assembly as a "little engine that could" . . . stop your car. Each brake assembly is an engine. It just works backward—so to speak—through friction. The brakes convert the energy of motion into heat, and dissipate that heat into the atmosphere. And here's an interesting little fact: The brakes on even the most mundane family car are far more powerful than its engine! Said differently, motor vehicles stop better than they go, which is always good news when there's a solid object in close proximity!

Believe it or not, many very early motor vehicles—perhaps motor carriages would be a better term—either had no brakes at all or relied upon a simple friction brake, not unlike the lever arm that rubbed on the wheel of your first go-kart (not a particularly efficient way to stop the vehicle). Of course these motorized carriages weren't very fast and there weren't many other vehicles or objects to hit, so motorists didn't have to worry too much about stopping quickly. As vehicle speeds climbed, the need to stop efficiently became increasingly important. Friction brakes and cable-operated mechanical brakes provided some stopping power, but were not consistently effective or reliable in stopping the vehicle quickly and safely.

HYDRAULIC BRAKES

Then came the birth of the hydraulic brake system, which is still the foundation of brake technology on today's automobiles. Research and development is leading the industry toward fly-by-wire automobiles, like modern aircraft, where the control inputs will be transmitted electronically to the control systems. That means perhaps future brake systems will not have a direct connection between your foot and the vehicle's brakes. Your foot will operate a rheostat or variable resistor that will send a variable electrical signal to a computer. The computer will figure out that you would really like to stop your vehicle and will command the individual brakes to apply the precise amount of brake force necessary to stop your car as you intend— hopefully.

No doubt we'll see the fly-by-wire systems in the near future, but until then our motor vehicles will

HYDRAULIC BRAKE SYSTEM

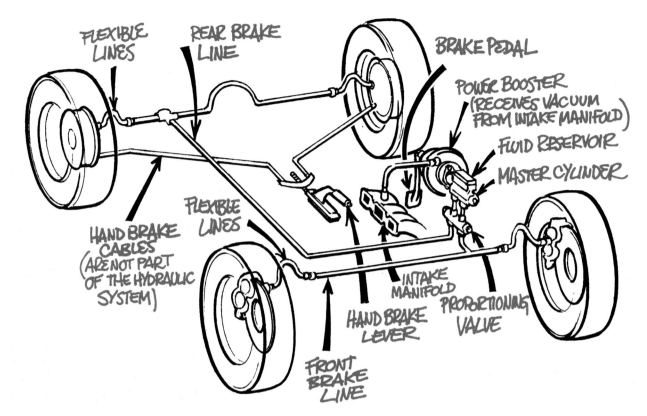

FLEXIBLE LINES

REAR BRAKE LINE

BRAKE PEDAL

POWER BOOSTER (RECEIVES VACUUM FROM INTAKE MANIFOLD)

FLUID RESERVOIR

MASTER CYLINDER

HAND BRAKE CABLES (ARE NOT PART OF THE HYDRAULIC SYSTEM)

FLEXIBLE LINES

INTAKE MANIFOLD

HAND BRAKE LEVER

PROPORTIONING VALVE

FRONT BRAKE LINE

continue to rely on hydraulic brakes to stop safely and reliably. Even with today's dual master cylinder disc brake systems equipped with antilock braking system (ABS), traction, and stability control, the basics of hydraulic brake systems have not changed over the decades.

WHY HYDRAULICS?

Because of a fundamental property of hydraulic fluid or oil, it is not compressible. When you apply pressure to the brake pedal in your vehicle, the pedal's mechanical linkage moves a pushrod in the master cylinder that forces a piston down the bore of that cylinder, which is filled with hydraulic fluid. The movement of that piston generates hydraulic pressure, which is transmitted through an interconnected series of brake lines—metallic pipes and flexible hoses—to the individual brake assemblies at each wheel. The pressure reaching the brake assembly at each wheel pushes the pistons in the brake caliper. Then the caliper squeezes the brake pads against the rotor, creating friction, generating heat, dissipating energy, and slowing the vehicle. In a drum brake assembly, the pressures moves the pistons in the wheel cylinder, which push the brake shoes outward against the inside surface of the brake drum, creating friction and heat, thus slowing the vehicle.

The harder you push the pedal, the more hydraulic pressure is generated in the system, the more force pushing the friction material against the rotors and/or drums, the faster the energy of motion is converted into heat . . . and the quicker your vehicle stops. Now you know how your brakes work!

The beauty of hydraulic brake system is its basic simplicity. The system has very few moving parts, is relatively self-contained and sealed, is remarkably consistent in operation, and is amazingly reliable. That's why it will take twenty-first century technology to ultimately replace hydraulic brakes with fly–by–wire brakes.

KEY COMPONENTS

Hydraulic fluid/oil—glycol or silicone-based fluid that is incompressible

Brake master cylinder—tandem dual circuit hydraulic cylinder, meaning one cylinder with two pistons; each circuit operates one-half the brake system; can be front/rear or diagonal right-front/left-rear, left-front/right-rear

Proportioning valve—hydraulic device that balances and/or limits hydraulic pressure to the rear brakes to prevent premature rear brake lockup; either incorporated into the master cylinder, or a separate valve in the rear brake hydraulic line

181

DISC BRAKES

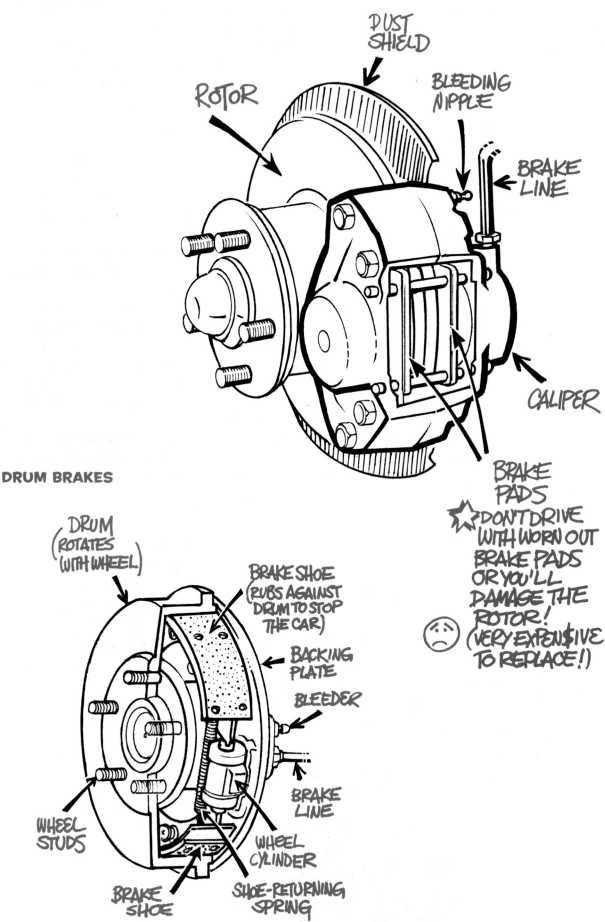

DUST SHIELD

ROTOR

BLEEDING NIPPLE

BRAKE LINE

CALIPER

BRAKE PADS

☆ DON'T DRIVE WITH WORN OUT BRAKE PADS OR YOU'LL DAMAGE THE ROTOR! (VERY EXPEN$IVE TO REPLACE!) ☹

DRUM BRAKES

DRUM (ROTATES WITH WHEEL)

BRAKE SHOE (RUBS AGAINST DRUM TO STOP THE CAR)

BACKING PLATE

BLEEDER

BRAKE LINE

WHEEL STUDS

WHEEL CYLINDER

BRAKE SHOE

SHOE-RETURNING SPRING

Power brake booster—vacuum or hydraulic device that assists you in applying pressure to the master cylinder; keeps brake pedal pressure requirements in the comfort range

Disc brake caliper—relatively simple hydraulic vice whose piston(s) squeezes the brake pads against the brake rotor when hydraulic pressure is applied, thus generating heat, dissipating energy, and slowing the vehicle; found on the front wheels of most cars and light trucks, and on all four wheels of higher performance vehicles; today, four-wheel disc brake systems are becoming the standard on almost all cars and trucks

Brake rotor or disc—flat cast-iron disc mounted on the wheel hub that rotates with the wheel, between the brake pads in the caliper; transfers the brake force to the wheel/tire to slow the vehicle

Brake pads—individual blocks of friction material glued onto a heavy, flat steel plate and mounted in the caliper like the two pieces of bread of a sandwich

Brake wheel cylinder—small hydraulic cylinder mounted inside the brake drum that pushes both brake shoes outward, into contact with the inside friction surface of the brake drum, generating heat, dissipating energy, and slowing the vehicle; not quite as efficient as disc brake

Brake drum—large cast-iron drum mounted on the wheel hub that rotates with the wheel and transfers the brake force to the wheel/tire

Brake shoe—friction material glued and/or riveted onto a curved shoe mounted inside the brake drum, and pivoted into contact with the inside surface of the brake drum by the wheel cylinder

ANTILOCK BRAKING SYSTEMS (ABS)

Okay, now that we've outlined how hydraulic brake systems work, answer this simple question: How well will the brakes stop the vehicle . . . if the tires are not touching the pavement? Not too well, sadly. The point to remember is that your desire to stop your vehicle is dependent upon not only the performance of the hydraulic brake system, but also the ability of the tires to transmit that into the pavement.

To optimize the stopping power of your vehicle in an emergency situation, the tires need to be slipping just a bit on the pavement. Literally, the tires need to be rotating right at the threshold of lockup, about 10 percent slower than road speed. This optimizes the traction of the tires, allowing maximum braking action and stopping power.

Can you threshold brake with your vehicle? Have you ever panic-braked trying to avoid something ahead of you, locked up the tires, and found that not only did

ANTI-LOCK BRAKE SYSTEMS (ABS)

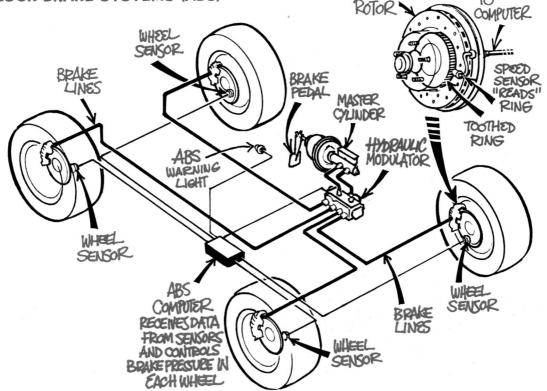

the vehicle not stop very well, but you also couldn't steer it at all? Think about an experience in slippery conditions, perhaps ice or snow, when you suddenly realized that you weren't stopping anywhere near as well as you'd like because the tires were sliding across the pavement.

Now, if you were a really, really good driver, you could have fixed that problem by modulating pressure on the brake pedal a bit. Incrementally reducing pressure until the wheels unlocked could have helped you regain grip so that you could have stopped efficiently or steered around the threat.

Unless you practice this on a regular basis, which wouldn't make you particularly popular with your neighbors, this is difficult to do—particularly in the heat of battle when you really, really, really need to stop before you hit that solid object. If you could threshold brake perfectly—applying exactly the right amount of pressure on the brake pedal to keep the tires at the very edge of optimum traction—you could bring your vehicle to a stop as quickly as the vehicle was capable of stopping.

But could you do this the very first time you needed to? When little Bobby pops out from between the parked cars, chasing his ball? Hopefully, but probably not.

Enter ABS—antilock braking system. In the simplest of terms, ABS is an electronic add-on to standard hydraulic brake systems. By monitoring the rotational speed of each wheel through a wheel speed sensor and feeding that information into a small microprocessor, the ABS system can recognize when you've pushed the brake pedal too hard and the tires are in the process of locking up. How does it know this? No, not by your screams behind the wheel. The system identifies that the rotational speed of one or more wheels is slowing faster than the others; that's the moment of impending brake lockup.

The ABS computer signals a hydraulic assembly to rapidly cycle hydraulic valves open and closed to the individual brake or brakes that are locking up. The cyclic and very rapid valve openings bleed off just enough hydraulic pressure to those brakes to keep them at the edge of optimum traction. Thus, the ABS system prevents you from over-braking—applying too much brake force, locking the wheels, loosing steering control, and reducing brake efficiency. Thank you very much!

Just think, the ABS is there fulltime, silently, unobtrusively, patiently waiting for you to push too hard on the brake pedal. Then the ABS leaps into action to save your bacon by preventing the wheels from locking up and you losing control of your vehicle. Does that qualify for hero status?

TRACTION AND STABILITY CONTROL

Traction and stability control systems carry the ABS concept a step or two further. By monitoring the rotational speeds of the drive wheels, traction control systems can reduce wheelspin in slippery conditions, thus improving drive traction and control. Some systems can apply the brake on the drive wheel that's spinning, while others reduce engine power electronically. Still others combine both features to minimize loss of drive traction in rain, snow, and ice.

Stability control systems add sensors that can detect yaw, when the direction the vehicle is pointed is not the same as the direction it is traveling—always an exciting moment and often a precursor to loss of control. The system applies a combination of individual brake action and reduction in engine power to help restabilize the vehicle. Hmm, and you thought you were a good driver!

But remember, even with all the sophistication and benefits of ABS and traction and stability control systems, the heart and soul of your vehicle's ability to stop safely is the hydraulic brake system and your right foot.

BRAKE SYSTEM MAINTENANCE

Brake pads and brake shoes are expendable components, meaning that they will wear out in normal use. The life expectancy of brake friction material varies depending as much on driving style and environment as it does on vehicle size and weight. That's why brake components should be inspected on a regular basis. When? At every oil change is a good plan. While the oil's draining, you or the technician should at least visually inspect the front brake pads, which are usually visible without removing the wheels. To help make sure you know when it's time for new brakes, little metal tabs are mounted on the edge of the brake pads that come into contact with the rotor when the pad is worn down to about 20 percent of its original thickness.

If you start to hear a light chirping sound as you turn the steering wheel or when you lightly apply the brakes, but the chirp stops if you squeeze the brake pedal harder, you are being officially notified that it's time to look at the brake pads.

When it's time for new brake pads, it's also time for a careful inspection of the brake rotors for scoring, run-out, out-of-round, and wear. Deep scoring can occur if you don't quite get to the pad replacement in time, and the friction material wears off the steel backing plate to the point that the backing plate contacts the rotor. Steel on cast iron often generates a nasty grinding sound and quickly ruins the rotor.

Can brake rotors be safely turned or machined (meaning the braking surface is ground smooth)? Sometimes yes, but often it is simpler, better, and more cost efficient to replace the rotor. Every brake rotor has a minimum thickness dimension stamped into the hub. If the rotor can be surfaced or turned to restore a perfectly smooth and uniform contact surface and still be above that minimum dimension, it might be worth turning. But if the wear is significant or the scoring, or grooving, is deep, replace the rotor.

Minor run-out, out-of-round, and rotor thickness variation are generally the result of normal wear and tear on rotors. How do you know if your brake rotors have problems? Symptoms—vibration in the brake pedal and/or steering wheel when you apply the brakes. The vibration is caused by the variation in the rotor surface as it rotates. The rotor literally pushes back against the brake pads; which push back against the piston in the caliper; which pushes back against the hydraulic fluid; which pushes back against the piston in the master cylinder; which pushes back against the brake pedal linkages; which cause the brake pedal to push back against your foot! Follow that?

If you've been experiencing some degree of vibration when the brakes are applied, expect to have to do something with the rotors, either turning or machining them to restore their flatness, or replacing them.

But the good news is that if it's time for new brake pads and the rotors are in good shape, all you need to do or have done is to scuff the surfaces of the rotors with a sanding disc to rough up the surface a bit. This will help the new brake pads bed, or seat, to the rotor to minimize squeal and noise and maximize stopping efficiency from the new pads.

Anytime new brake friction material is installed, it needs to be safely heat-cycled a few times. This is to boil the excess bonding agent off the surface of the friction material and help the pad or shoe conform to the surface of the rotor or drum. Often, this will occur in normal driving, but many brake shops will intentionally heat the brakes by repeated heavy applications—in a safe driving environment, of course—to quickly bed new brake pads to the rotor. Doing so helps reduce the

number of customers who return complaining of squeaky brakes.

Can you bed your own new brakes? Yes, as long as you do so safely. Find a long stretch of medium speed roadway—a 45-mile-per-hour speed limit works well. Accelerate gently to 30 miles per hour, and making sure no other vehicles are right behind you, brake firmly down to walking speed without locking the wheels. Re-accelerate back up to speed slowly to give the pads and rotors time to cool. Repeat the process about 20 times, then cruise along to cool the brakes.

What about drum brakes? A number of light trucks and passenger cars still utilize drum brake systems on the rear wheels. Why? Drum brakes are simple and inexpensive, but more importantly, because of the significant weight transfer forward when braking, the rear brakes on a motor vehicle do a much smaller percentage of the total braking action. So even though drum brakes aren't quite as efficient at dissipating heat as disc brakes, they are perfectly serviceable on the rear wheels of many vehicles.

Since it's not possible to see the brake shoes inside the brake drum in most cases, the drums should be removed at every tire rotation to inspect the shoes, wheels cylinders, and brake hardware.

BRAKE FLUID MAINTENANCE?

If you check the owner's manual for many high-end cars, you'll find a service recommendation to change the brake fluid periodically. This is an excellent maintenance suggestion even if you're driving a low-end car or truck. Like most other fluids in a modern automobile, brake fluid should be changed on a regular basis to maintain its performance and to minimize corrosion in the hydraulic system.

Historically, the fluid or oil utilized in hydraulic brake systems is glycol based. By its very nature this fluid is hygroscopic, meaning it will absorb moisture from the atmosphere. Now here's the key point: moisture is a very bad thing in brake fluid. Not only will moisture promote corrosion in calipers, wheel cylinders, master cylinders, ABS solenoids, and other expensive brake components, but even the smallest percentage of moisture in brake fluid will lower its boiling point significantly. And that means the potential for dreaded brake fade increases dramatically.

Brake Fade

Brake fade doesn't happen often, but when it does, it will grab your complete attention. The scenario may be something like this. You're headed down a long, continuous grade and need to apply modest pressure on the brake pedal repeatedly to prevent the vehicle from accelerating well beyond the safe and legal limit. As you continue down the grade, you begin to notice the pedal is beginning to travel closer to the floor each time you apply the brakes. Ultimately, the pedal may end up hitting the floor and you'll need to start pumping the pedal to restore any stopping power!

This type of brake fade is caused by the moisture in the fluid in the calipers and/or wheel cylinders actually beginning to boil. As it boils, the moisture turns into a vapor or gas, which is compressible. Thus, when you push the pedal, much if not all of its travel is consumed compressing the gas in the system rather than generating hydraulic pressure on the friction material.

Once the brake system has cooled down again, the pedal may fully return to normal. But often, the system will require bleeding to remove trapped air to restore a firm, solid, and confidence-inspiring brake pedal.

That's why it is worth replacing the brake fluid in your automobile every two years. The process is simple. Use a large syringe or turkey-baster to empty all but the last 1/8-inch of fluid from both chambers of the master cylinder reservoir. Refill the system with new brake fluid, then bleed the system until all the original fluid has been exchanged for new. Not only is the system now filled with fresh, clean, moisture-free brake fluid for optimum performance, but also any moisture and debris have been flushed from the system.

Here's the simple promise. Replacing the brake fluid every two years will help your vehicle stop better and more consistently, and expensive brake components will last longer. ■

BRAKE SYSTEM TROUBLESHOOTING

PROBLEM	PROBABLE CAUSES	ACTION TO REPAIR
BRAKE WARNING LIGHT ILLUMINATED	Low brake fluid level	Check brake fluid level. Add fliud if necessary. If fluid is low, have professional inspect brake system for fluid leakage. *(Project 43: Check Brake Fluid Level)*
	Hydraulic pressure loss/imbalance in brake system	Have professional check/test brake system Loss of hydraulic pressure in brake system presents a serious safety issue. Have vehicle towed to shop if possible.
	Parking brake mechanism stuck or not fully released	Check that parking brake is fully released. Check for binding/sticking in parking brake cable/linkage. *(Project 45: Replace rotors and Pads)*
SQUEAL WHEN APPLYING BRAKES	Minor "glazing"/buildup of bonding agent on brake pad and rotors	Lightly sand pads/scuff rotors to reseat brake pads. If squeal persists, have brake pads/rotors inspected by professional. *(Project 45: Replace rotors and Pads)*
HEAVY GRINDING NOISE WHEN APPLYING BRAKES	Worn out brake pads and/or shoes; metal-on-metal contact between pad backing plate and rotor	Replace pads and rotors (disc brakes); replace brake shoes and have drums resurfaced (drum brakes). *(Project 45: Replace rotors and Pads)*

BRAKE SYSTEM TROUBLESHOOTING

PROBLEM	PROBABLE CAUSES	ACTION TO REPAIR
DARK DUST ON SIDES OF VEHICLE OR ON WHEEL HUBS	Metallic debris from brake pad and rotor wear	Check brake pad wear and replace if necessary. **Note:** Some brake dust will regularly appear on modern cars with alloy wheels; this may not indicate your brake pads need to be replaced. (*Project 45: Replace rotors and Pads*)
LIGHT SQUEAL FROM BRAKES EVEN WHEN NOT APPLYING BRAKES—NOISE STOPS WHEN BRAKES APPLIED	Brake wear indicator tabs contacting rotor	Check brake pad wear and replace if necessary. (*Project 45: Replace rotors and Pads*)
LOW, FIRM BRAKE PEDAL	Misadjusted rear drum brakes	Apply foot brake repeatedly while safely backing up slowly. Manually adjust shoes
	Misadjusted rear disc brakes; failure to use parking brake to keep rear disc brake calipers properly adjusted	To adjust, repeatedly apply parking brake while braking lightly at low speed
BRAKE PEDAL REQUIRES EXTRA EFFORT TO PRESS, IS SOMEWHAT MUSHY, AND/OR REQUIRES SEVERAL STROKES TO GET BRAKES TO APPLY	Brake power assist not functioning	Brakes are either vacuum-assisted or hydraulically assisted. Your owner's manual should list which type your car has **Vacuum-assisted brakes** Shut off engine, pump brake pedal If no difference in pedal effort, power assist is gone, immediately check hose/valve connections to power brake booster for vacuum leak **Hydraulically assisted brakes** Check operation of hydraulic pump/fluid/drive belt (note that most hydraulically assisted brake systems get hydraulic power from the power steering pump)
	Air trapped in brake system	Bleed brakes to expel air. If problem reappears, have professional check hydraulic brake system. Possible faulty master cylinder/caliper/wheel cylinder

BRAKE SYSTEM TROUBLESHOOTING

PROBLEM	PROBABLE CAUSES	ACTION TO REPAIR
VEHICLE "PULLS" WHEN BRAKES APPLIED	Hydraulic problem with caliper/ master cylinder	Have brake hydralics tested and, if necessary, repaired at local brake shop
	Uneven hydraulic pressure from master cylinder	Check/replace master cylinder, bleed brakes
	Stuck caliper piston/slider; overheated front brake from stuck caliper	Replace brake caliper, bleed brakes
	Tire problem (see Tire & Wheel Troubleshooting chart)	
	Wheel alignment problem (see Suspension/ Steering Troubleshooting chart)	
VIBRATION/PULSATION IN BRAKE PEDAL	Rotors/drums warped, run-out, out of round, rotor thickness variation	Inspect, service, and replace brake components
	Distorted brake rotor from uneven wheel lug torque	Properly torque wheel lugs
	NOTE: Anti-lock brake systems (ABS) can generate a chatter or pulsation in the brake pedal when it is activated. Read owner's manual for details on your car	
POOR BRAKING PERFORMANCE	Lack of rear brake action	Have professional inspect/service brake system
	Lack of front brake action	Have professional inspect/service brake system
ABS LIGHT ILLUMINATED	Full-time ABS light indicated problem/failure with ABS	Have professional troubleshoot fault codes from PCM

Check Brake Fluid Level

TALENT:	1
TIME:	5 minutes
TOOLS:	None
COST:	$0
TIP:	Keep brake fluid off paint finish.

1 The brake fluid reservoir lies on top of the brake master cylinder, which is typically bolted to the firewall on the driver's side above the brake pedal.

2 Sometimes it's easier to see the fluid level if you remove the cap (see photo on opposite page). The fluid shows through this reservoir nicely. It is marked for minimum and full levels. Remember, the fluid level in this reservoir will drop a bit in normal operation as the friction material on the brake pads and shoes wears away. More fluid will be drawn into the system to take up the slack as caliper and wheel cylinder pistons extend farther to apply brake pressure.

3 To top up the fluid level, pour in brake fluid of the proper specification as noted in your owner's manual. Most brake fluid attracts water and should be changed periodically to avoid corrosion in the system.

TIP: If your brake fluid is low, it may indicate a system leak in need of attention.

Project 44
Replace Brake Drums and Shoes

TALENT: 4

TIME: 60–120 minutes

TOOLS: Socket wrench, pliers

COST: $60–$100

TIP: If you forget how it all goes back together, you can remove the drum on the other side and use that brake as a model. Or take a digital photo as soon as you remove the drum.

1 Break the rear lug nuts free, then jack up the rear end of the vehicle and place safely up on jack stands. (See sidebar in Chapter 1 for a quick explanation of how to jack up your car.)

2 Slide the drum off the wheel studs. If it sticks, tap it lightly around the rim with a hammer. Be careful, cast-iron drums can crack. Try putting a board against the drum and tapping the board. If the drum is rusted or stuck on the wheel studs or centering hole, hammer squarely on the wheel mating surface to break the drum free. On some vehicles, the drum may be retained by a screw.

TIP: After the car is jacked up and resting on jack stands, release the emergency/parking brake, otherwise it will hold the drum on.

3 Remove the shoe retaining clips, which are spring-loaded. With a strong hand, you can remove these with pliers, though auto parts stores sell an inexpensive special tool that makes this much easier.

4a Remove the shoe return springs, which attach one brake shoe to another. On some vehicles it's easier to remove the top spring(s) first; in others it's easier to start with the bottom spring(s). On this Dodge Stratus, the bottom spring is easier. Locking pliers make this job easier, too.

4b

5a Here's another brake drum with a different spring setup for comparison. Note the round shoe retaining clips here.

TIP: Brake springs can rust and break. Buy a brake-spring kit when you replace the brakes. Open the kit and figure out the placement and orientation of each new spring before you remove the old ones.

5b

6 With the springs removed, the shoes will separate.

7 The rearward shoe will typically be attached to a linkage and cable running to your parking/emergency brake. Use a pliers to push back its spring retainer and remove the cable from the brake shoe.

8 With the retaining clips, spring, and parking brake cable removed, lift off the brake shoes. Make sure no one touches the brake pedal with the drums off, and make sure the wheel cylinder pistons don't extend out too far as you remove the shoes.

Once the shoes are off, peel back the edge of the rubber boots on each end of the wheel cylinder to check for brake fluid and evidence of leaks.

9 When you brake, the shoes get pushed into the drums.

10 Installing the new drums and pads is the reverse of removing the old ones.

Project 45

Replace Brake Rotors and Pads

TALENT: 4

TIME: 60–90 minutes

TOOLS: Pliers, socket wrench, screwdriver, length of wire to hang caliper

COST: $25–$60

TIP: For more advanced repairs, a factory service manual is invaluable. A dealership can order one for your make and model.

1 With the car on the ground, break the lug nuts free, jack up the front end of the car, and place it safely on jack stands. (See the Sidebar in Chapter 1 for a quick explanation of how to jack up your car.)

caliper

rotor

2 Remove the wheel and loosen the nuts or bolts securing the brake caliper, which holds the pads. A special tool or socket, often a hex drive, may be necessary.

3 Use a screwdriver to carefully lever the inboard pad back just a bit to create clearance between the pads and rotor (brake disc). Now remove the retaining bolts and lift the caliper off of the rotor.

4 Hang the caliper from the front suspension with a piece of wire so there is no stress on the brake hose.

5 Pull the rotor off of the wheel studs.

Note: Some rotors are part of, or even riveted to, the hub and may require disassembly and repacking of the front wheel bearings. Check at your auto parts supplier about the specific setup for your vehicle. Repacking bearings requires skill and precision and may be more than you want to tackle.

6 Pry the brake pads from the caliper, taking great care not to damage the piston and its protective rubber boot. Some pads have clips, some have indentations and ridges holding them in place, and some have tabs that are crimped in place. Study the pad and caliper and you'll discover how to remove it.

7 Here are several brake pads in various conditions.

Pads on the right: The thicker one is fine. The other is just about at the end of its life. A shorthand rule is that 1/4 inch thick is okay, but 1/8 inch is ready to be replaced. Below 1/8 inch, the pads should be replaced immediately to avoid reduced braking efficiency and more costly repairs.

Pads on the left: These pads are both thin and glazed. Glazing is a sort of polishing of the pad, which reduces its coefficient of friction and braking efficiency.

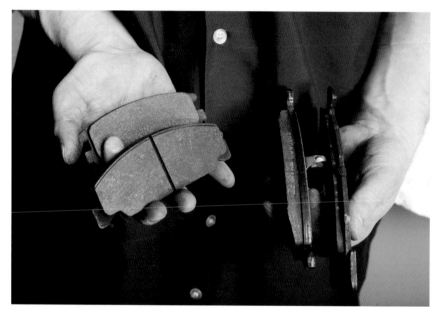

8 Before installing new pads, you'll need to force the caliper piston back into the caliper to create space for the new, thicker pad. Use a large C-clamp pushing against the old brake pad to push the piston all the way back into the caliper. Do this slowly, smoothly, and carefully to ensure the piston doesn't cock or wedge into the caliper bore.

Note: As you do this, it's a good idea to push a rubber hose over the bleeder screw, aim it into a small container, and open the bleeder screw just a bit to allow fluid to escape as you push the caliper piston back. This prevents brake fluid from being pushed back toward the ABS unit and master cylinder, potentially carrying any moisture, corrosion, or debris into these sensitive, expensive components.

Note: If you're changing the brake pads on the rear calipers, you may need a special tool that rotates the piston as it is pushed back into the caliper. This resets the ratchet mechanism operated by the parking brake. Failing to rotate the piston can permanently damage this mechanism. You can rent or purchase this tool from most auto parts stores.

9 Reinstall the new rotor and pads in reverse order of disassembly. Take apart only one wheel's brakes at a time, so if you get confused you can refer to the other side for part placement and orientation.

Mount the new pads securely in both halves of the caliper, as per instructions. Reinstall the caliper on its mount, and firmly tighten the caliper mounting bolts. Tightening them to the proper specification with a torque wrench is always a good idea.

Once the new pads and caliper are installed properly, push the brake pedal several times to move the new pads into contact with the rotors, and to make sure you've got a solid, firm brake pedal.

Project 46
Bleed Brake System

TALENT: 3

TIME: 45–60 minutes

TOOLS: Combination wrench, hose, container

COST: Brake fluid $6–$8

TIP: Brake fluid is hygroscopic, which means it absorbs water. Use a new, sealed bottle for best results, and discard old fluid according to local regulations.

1 On the back side of the brake drum and the brake caliper, there is a brake bleeder screw or nipple. The one in this photo is fitted with a rubber cap to prevent dirt from entering it. Remove the cap if present. To make sure the bleeder screw opens easily, apply a drop of penetrating lubricant or spray. It's very easy to break off a bleeder screw, so take your time and use a box-end wrench.

2 Place the wrench on the bleeder screw and fit a length of clear tubing over the nipple. Place the other end in a container filled with a small amount of brake fluid. Have an assistant sit in the driver's seat with a window open so he or she can hear you.

3 Start with the brake farthest from the master cylinder, usually the right rear. Then in sequence bleed the left rear, right front, and finally the left front caliper. Follow this bleeding sequence at least twice to fully bleed the system and exchange all the old brake fluid for new, fresh fluid.

The procedure to bleed each brake is as follows:

1) Tell the assistant to pump the brake pedal.

2) After several pumps —at three or four full strokes of the pedal— say "hold."

3) The assistant holds the pedal at the bottom of its travel while you open the bleeder screw. Liquid and air will bubble out.

4) Tighten the screw.

5) Say "up," or "release," so your assistant will release the pedal.

6) Repeat the process several times on each brake until only clean fluid with no air bubbles comes out during step three.

4 As you bleed the system, the reservoir will empty. Check it and top it up after bleeding each brake assembly to ensure that it doesn't run dry, as this will draw air back into the system, and you'll have to start the process all over again.

Chapter 10
Exhaust

⚠ WARNING!

🔆 KEY CONCEPT

📯 OLD SCHOOL TECH

🔧 MAINTENANCE TIP

🛸 TOMORROW'S TECH

🐷 MONEY-SAVING TIP

For most vehicle owners, the exhaust system is a non-factor. Many carmakers now use aluminized stainless steel in the construction of the tailpipes and mufflers installed on their vehicles. This corrosion-resistant material makes the entire exhaust system almost a life-of-the-vehicle component.

That's good news for car owners. The words "exhaust," "muffler," and "tailpipe" generally never even cross our minds, until we suddenly hear a loud, roaring sound as the muffler splits open or breaks away from the tailpipe. Sometimes this is followed by loud screeching sounds as the muffler or pipe drag along the highway. Even though the exhaust system on our automobile is way down our priority list in terms of importance, it's actually a key system in the safe, efficient, and quiet operation of our vehicles.

EXHAUST 101

The basic idea behind the exhaust system is to direct the hot, loud exhaust gases produced by the combustion process in the engine through the exhaust manifold. This is typically a cast-iron exhaust collector bolted directly to the engine's cylinder head, into a sealed length of tubing, through a muffler, and finally through a tailpipe to the very back of the car.

The goal is simple: carry the potentially noxious exhaust to the rear and dump it into the atmosphere behind the vehicle. Along the way, route it through a muffler to absorb a large percentage of the audible sound of combustion to quiet the exhaust to a level that allows reasonable conversation and sanity inside the cabin.

CATALYTIC CONVERTER

And with the modern automotive era, there's one more important job for the exhaust: clean the exhaust gases of unburned hydrocarbons. This is accomplished by adding one more component to the system, the catalytic converter. This device is a muffler-like housing filled with a special material the helps oxidize/burn any gasoline that may have exited the engine unburned. The material used for catalytic converters is platinum or palladium, both precious metals with the unique characteristic of being able to be heated to extraordinary temperatures to help finish the burn process of the air/fuel mixture exiting the engine. The results of this catalyst is to reduce the hydrocarbon (HC) emissions from the tailpipe.

OXYGEN SENSORS

Modern motor vehicles also incorporate one more component in the exhaust system: a small oxygen sensor mounted between the engine and the catalytic converter. This little electronic gizmo compares the percentage of oxygen in the exhaust with the percentage of oxygen in the atmosphere, generates a

THE EXHAUST SYSTEM

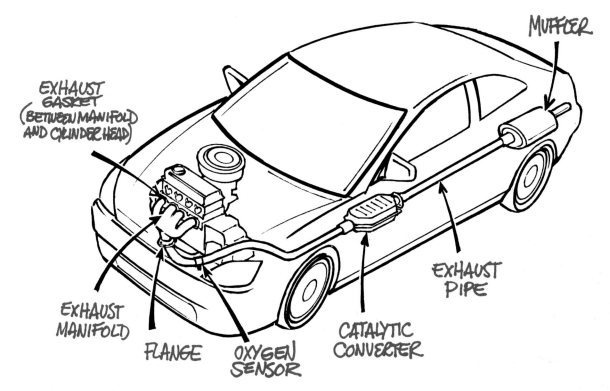

EXHAUST GASKET (BETWEEN MANIFOLD AND CYLINDER HEAD)

EXHAUST MANIFOLD

FLANGE

OXYGEN SENSOR

CATALYTIC CONVERTER

EXHAUST PIPE

MUFFLER

low voltage signal representing that ratio, and feeds that signal to the engine management computer hundreds of times per second. The signal from the oxygen sensor allows the PCM to trim the fuel delivery for optimum performance, efficiency, and minimum emissions.

Since about 1995 or 1996, the oxygen sensors and the entire engine management system have become more sophisticated, and now include a second oxygen sensor behind the catalytic converter. This sensor monitors catalyst efficiency to help confirm that the front oxygen sensor is doing a good job of reducing the percentage of unburned fuel in the exhaust, i.e. maintaining an optimal air/fuel ratio, and thus reducing the workload on the catalytic converter.

EXHAUST MAINTENANCE

In terms of maintenance and repair, exhaust system components, in large part, fall into the "if it ain't broke, don't fix it" category—always popular with car owners (with the exception of the oxygen sensors which will be covered later in this chapter). Obviously, the complete exhaust system needs to be intact and sealed to properly do its job of quieting the engine to a tolerable level, protecting occupants from exhaust gases and carbon monoxide entering the cabin, catalyzing any unburned fuel, and providing the oxygen sensor signal

to the PCM. Any physical damage or leaks need to be corrected right away.

DIAGNOSIS AND CAUSES OF EXHAUST FAILURE

How will you know when there's a problem? Oh, couldn't hear me over the sound of the engine. . . . Trust me, you'll know! The exhaust note will increase in decibels and sharpness. You'll think a locomotive is about to run you over! The engine will sound louder, particularly under acceleration, and even as you coast or slow down, you may hear popping sounds from the exhaust. Any time you note a change in sound from the exhaust, have the entire exhaust system inspected for damage or leaks.

Where would damage to the exhaust system come from? Driving along at night and running over the cinderblock you never saw might do the trick. Large objects going under the vehicle can physically break, crush, and pinch off exhaust pipes and mufflers.

But the primary cause for exhaust failure is good ol' rust—corrosion with a capital C. Not only is the outside of the exhaust vulnerable to moisture, salt, dirt, sand, and other road debris that can generate rust, but also

VROOooM!!! KPOW!!!

the primary byproducts of the internal combustion engine are water and combustion acids. These collect in the exhaust system and eat away at the metal. That's why the mild steel exhaust pipes and mufflers used for so many generations of motor vehicles rusted away faster than ice melting in tea on a hot summer day. In fact, if you live in the rust belt, where acid rain and road salt are the number one enemies of automobiles, you may well be able to hear your exhaust system rusting away on a quiet day (hopefully you have something better to do, though).

Often, the corrosion will make itself known first at the lowest point in the complete exhaust system. This may be at a bend in the exhaust or tailpipe, or a seam in the muffler. Once rust starts, it's just a matter of time.

That's why replacing a rusted muffler with a new one carrying a lifetime guarantee isn't a bad idea. And ask the shop to drill a tiny 1/8-inch hole in the lowest part of the muffler; this will help drain the moisture/water that collects in the muffler, and can help prolong the muffler's life.

REPLACEMENT ADVICE

If and when you are forced to replace exhaust components, please remember the old adage: You get what you pay for. The cheapest mufflers and tailpipes

may quiet your vehicle down again, but thin-wall mild steel will rust pretty quickly, particularly in areas where salt is used on the roadways in winter. You may well be better off to have top quality exhaust components carrying a lifetime warranty installed, particularly if you're planning to keep the vehicle for at least another three to five years.

Even though the replacement components are guaranteed for as long as you own your car, expect to pay for new hangers, clamps, and in some cases, new sections of pipe if your lifetime muffler fails.

The exhaust manifold bolted to the cylinder head generally never needs service or replacement. The cast iron is well suited to the thousands of heat cycles, from cold-at-startup to carrying 1,400-degree Fahrenheit exhaust gases out of the engine. Occasionally, an exhaust manifold will warp or crack, creating a very sharp exhaust leak that sounds very much like an ignition spark arcing to ground—a snapping sound that's amplified during acceleration. If this occurs, a new exhaust manifold is necessary. While it may be possible to weld up a crack, it's probably not worth the time, effort, or risk of recracking.

OXYGEN SENSOR MAINTENANCE

There are two exhaust system components that do need maintenance. Many carmakers call for oxygen sensor replacement at specific mileage intervals,

THE CATALYTIC CONVERTER

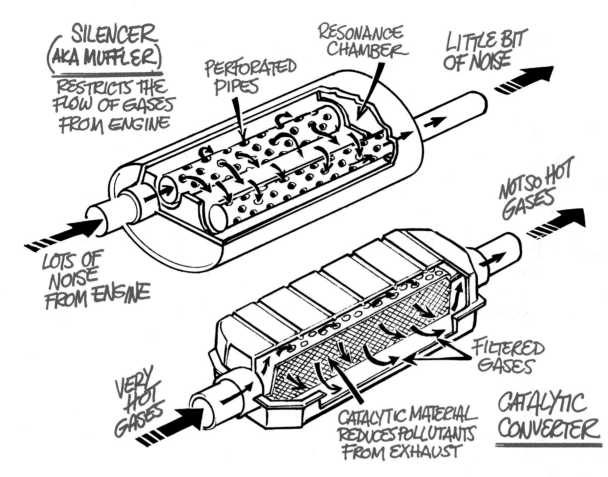

SILENCER (AKA MUFFLER) — RESTRICTS THE FLOW OF GASES FROM ENGINE

PERFORATED PIPES

RESONANCE CHAMBER

LITTLE BIT OF NOISE

LOTS OF NOISE FROM ENGINE

NOT SO HOT GASES

VERY HOT GASES

FILTERED GASES

CATALYTIC MATERIAL REDUCES POLLUTANTS FROM EXHAUST

CATALYTIC CONVERTER

typically in the 75,000–125,000-mile range. Why? Because the sensor's performance deteriorates with age. It's cross-count rate—the speed at which it recognizes the changes in oxygen percentage in the exhaust and signals the PCM—can slow down to the point where the engine management system cannot optimize the air/fuel ratio. The symptoms are very subtle; unless you check your fuel mileage regularly and accurately, you may never recognize the 1 or 2 mile-per-gallon loss in fuel economy from a sluggish oxygen sensor.

In many ways, replacing the oxygen sensor(s) between the engine and catalytic converter is the best tune-up a modern vehicle with 100,000 miles can have. Replacing a sluggish oxygen sensor will certainly deliver the most noticeable improvement in performance and economy. With continually rising fuel costs, make sure you have the oxygen sensor's performance and cross-count rate checked at your 100,000-mile tune-up, when fresh spark plugs are installed.

Replacing an oxygen sensor isn't difficult and can be a DIY project. Most sensors have the same hex-size as an old spark plug at 13/16 inch. A large open-end box wrench and a large quantity of aerosol penetrant usually do the job. With the system relatively cool, locate and liberally spray the boss, or thread, of the oxygen sensor with the penetrant. Repeat several more times, even over a several-day period. Then, when you're ready—properly gloved and wearing eye protection—and the vehicle is in a safe position to allow you access and leverage, unplug the sensor, mount the wrench, and apply firm pressure—which means push as hard as you can. Never pull the wrench toward you, unless you are looking forward to a new set of front teeth. If you can break the sensor loose, just unscrew it from the pipe, install the replacement, plug it into the harness, and you're on your way. You've just tuned-up you car!

In post-1995 vehicles fitted with front and rear oxygen sensors, the oxygen sensor behind the catalytic converter does not need replacing unless it fails. Ditto the catalytic converter. Although there is some evidence that catalytic converter performance degrades over tens of thousands of miles, no carmaker calls for periodic replacement.

But catalytic converters do fail. They can be killed by excessively rich air/fuel mixtures, which feed too much raw, unburned fuel into the converters. This causes the converter to work much harder at much higher temperatures to oxidize the unburned fuel. Have you ever smelled that nasty rotten egg smell from the exhaust on your vehicle? It's not uncommon to smell a tinge of this in the first few moments after a cold start, but once the car is up to full operating temperature, you really shouldn't have to apologize to your passengers by claiming, "It wasn't me, it's the car!"

Catalytic converters that consistently operate at higher-than-normal temperatures to do their job of catalyzing unburned fuel tend to fail prematurely. Often, it's a mechanical failure of the matrix or beehive-like structure inside. Once this brittle material begins to crumble, it can lead to blockage of exhaust flow, overheated exhaust manifolds, and a significant loss of power and fuel economy.

EMISSIONS WARRANTIES

By the way, did you know that the federal government mandates an emissions warranty on every new vehicle, and has since the 1980s? Until the mid-1990s and the introduction of OBDII engine management systems, the federal emissions warranty was five years/50,000 miles for emissions components, including the catalytic converter. Since 1995–1996, the federal warranty has increased to eight years/80,000 miles, with specific coverage for the computer and catalytic converter.

HEAT SHIELD FAILURE

One other component, part of the catalytic converter, tends to fail on modern exhaust systems. It's the heat shield, which protects the converter from coming into contact with flammable materials like leaves and newspapers. Remember the extraordinarily high temperatures the converter can reach as it oxidizes unburned fuel? That's why the heat shield is mounted on the converter to stand off any debris and prevent its physical contact with the converter.

Ever notice the large clam- or crab-shell-like pieces of metal lying on the side of the road? Yep, these are rusted heat shields that have broken off catalytic converters. Guess it's a good thing most of us don't park on top of leaf piles, eh?

With the thousands of heat cycles from startup to shut-down, engine vibrations traveling through the exhaust, and all the road bumps and potholes that jolt the chassis, it's no wonder these heat shields tend to break away and drop off after many years and tens of thousands of miles. Oh yeah, don't forget to add rust to the equation; this problem is more pronounced in rust belt states.

You may actually have some warning that the heat shield is going to fail—a pronounced, annoying buzz or rattle, typically noticeable under specific circumstances like at a stoplight idling in gear. If you catch it before it breaks completely off, it might be possible to reweld or steel-strap the heat shield back in place. Do you know anyone who has ever had this done? Probably not.

And speaking of legal, car owners in specific cities and regions in 35 states must have the emission systems in their vehicles inspected and/or tested periodically—usually every other year. The typical testing standard is the I/M240 inspection and maintenance test, which involves operating the vehicle on a chassis dynamometer while a special probe samples and analyzes the exhaust emissions. A visual inspection confirms that the entire exhaust system is intact, including the catalytic converter, and that the fuel filler cap is in place. ∎

EXHAUST SYSTEM TROUBLESHOOTING

PROBLEM	PROBABLE CAUSES	ACTION TO REPAIR
LOUD ROAR FROM UNDERNEATH CAR—GETS LOUDER WHEN YOU STEP ON THE GAS PRESENT WHETHER OR NOT CAR IS MOVING	Broken or rusted exhaust pipe	Replace pipe
	Broken or rusted exhaust muffler	Replace muffler
	Broken exhaust manifold	Replace exhaust manifold
SNAPPING SOUND UNDER HOOD	Blown exhaust manifold gasket	Replace exhaust manifold gasket
	Cracked or broken exhaust manifold	Replace exhaust manifold
	Spark from ignition plug wire arcing to ground	Replace spark plug wires
LOUD SCRAPING SOUND COMING FROM UNDERNEATH YOUR CAR	Dragging exhaust component	Temporarily wire up safely with coat hanger
		Break off loose piece to safely drive car to shop
		⚠ Park vehicle in safe location to do this
LOSS OF ENGINE POWER	Restricted exhaust and/or clogged/blocked muffler or catalytic converter	Check for exhaust exiting at tailpipe. Put gloved hand close to (but not ON) tailpipe outlet and feel for exhaust pulses exiting the tailpipe. If little or no exhaust flow, take to muffler repair shop for diagnosis and repair
	Crimped or bent exhaust pipe	Crawl under car and inspect for bent pipe replace if necessary.
		⚠ Park vehicle in safe location to do this. Do not support vehicle on jack for this "fix"
PHFFT SOUND FROM UNDER VEHICLE	Small exhaust leak from pipe/muffler/connection	For quick/cheap fix, try repairing with exhaust tape available at auto parts store; more permanent fix will most likely be required at muffler shop

Chapter 11
Caring for Car Interior and Exterior

☠ WARNING!	❗ KEY CONCEPT
OLD SCHOOL TECH	🔧 MAINTENANCE TIP
TOMORROW'S TECH	🐷 MONEY-SAVING TIP

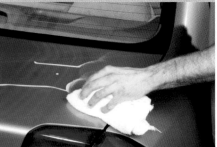

Having a clean, shiny vehicle in your driveway isn't just a personal feel-good and a fun way to keep the neighbors envious, it's the best way to preserve the appearance and value of your automobile. Ask any car dealer, new or used, and they'll tell you that initial appearance and impression are the number one assets when selling a motor vehicle. Besides, why drive a car or truck for years, then clean it up just in time to sell?

The basic maintenance schedule for a clean vehicle is to take advantage of the low-cost carwashes available with a fill-up at many convenience stores/gas stations. Every couple of times you fill up your tank, pay the extra few bucks and drive the vehicle through the carwash. While the touch-less carwashes don't clean the car perfectly, they do get the outer layer of crud off the painted surfaces. This is particularly critical if you drive in the snow belt, where salt and sand are used to clear the roadways in winter.

But the automatic carwash isn't enough. It doesn't remove dirt, grime, mud, salt, and sand from the truly vulnerable areas of your vehicle, the exact places rust starts! And remember this axiom: Rust never sleeps. To paraphrase a famous quote from an industrial engineer: "Ferrous metals prefer to exist in an oxidized state. Left to their own in our environment, they will rust into dust." That accurately describes what happens to sheet metal and steel stampings used to build automobiles. Just look at 10-year or older vehicles driven in the rust belt. Virtually all of them show the bubbled paint and rust-covered holes from corrosion. Granted, today's automobiles are better engineered, better built, and feature more galvanized metal, so they tend to resist rust better. But remember the axiom, if it's made of ferrous metal, it will eventually rust.

Also remember that you cannot prevent rust, but you can slow it down. That's what the paint on your automobile is for. Yes, we know, you thought that fire-engine red color was hot and would attract the attention of those you'd like to attract. But in reality, regardless of the color, the paint's job is to protect the steel and slow the process of corrosion on your wheeled fashion statement. The lesson here is simple: keep your vehicle clean, inside and out, top and bottom, and it will look better and last longer.

CARWASH 101

Once per month or so—more often if you drive on dirt/salty/sandy roads, in winter, near the ocean, or any other highly corrosive environment—wash the vehicle yourself, or pay to have it washed professionally.

CLEAN CARS MOVE FAST

Let's define a professional wash as the process of not only thoroughly cleaning the exposed painted surfaces, but flushing/washing the inner fenders, fender wells, inside edges of doors, hood and trunk, bumpers and valance panels, and underside of the chassis. Lots of high-pressure hot water works wonders at this task, which means the coin operated carwash is the best do-it-yourself tool for the task. Just make sure you bring plenty of quarters, because it will take more than one wash/rinse cycle to do the job right.

The Home Wash

Can you do as effective a job in your driveway at home? Yes, if you're willing to take the time. Connect your hose to the hot water outlet in the mud/laundry room if possible. Make sure you're using an automotive carwash product, and not laundry or dish detergent. These household products are too strong for the paint on your vehicle. If they can remove last night's baked-on lasagna from the dishes and that nasty grease stain from your work shirt, recognize that they will strip the oils and life right out of the paint.

A good bucket, wash mitt or big sponge, and the spray nozzle for your hose are all you need for the job. Oh yeah, and a handful of clean old towels. Thoroughly flush the entire car from top to bottom, including the underside, fender wells, and inside edges of the doors and door jams.

Speaking of doors, remember that the typical construction of an automotive door is to fold and crimp the door skin around the door frame, leaving the inside

edges vulnerable to rust. First, with the door open, flush the inside edges of the doors with hot water. Lift any seals or gaskets out of the way allow the spray to thoroughly flush away any accumulated crud. Then wipe the edges with your soapy sponge, and flush again. Repeat for each door, and don't forget the inner edges of the hood, trunk, tailgate, and gas filler cap.

Now, flush the underside of the chassis and fender wells—particularly the inner edge of the fender lips. Aim the hot water spray at the inside of the bumpers and valance panels, and walk the spray along the underside of the rocker panels along each side of the vehicle.

Open the hood and trunk, and carefully flush the edges and gasket/seal mating surfaces; then wipe them clean with your soapy sponge and flush again. You can even flush the inner fenders and lower portion of the firewall from inside the engine compartment; just don't aim the high pressure spray directly at sensitive engine electronics.

Once you've flushed the car, it's time to wash. Simple enough, just make sure the painted surfaces are thoroughly wet, use lots of your automotive carwash, and rinse your sponge/glove frequently to remove any solid debris. Wash in sections from the top down, rinse frequently, and keep finished sections wet until you've completed the entire job.

Once clean, put those nice dry, fluffy towels to work. You might want to buy and use an automotive squeegee to wipe the excess water away before drying in order to get more mileage from your towels. Dry thoroughly, including all the trim and bright work. Make sure all the glass is spotless, and lift the wiper blades off the windshield to wipe their contact edges clean.

To finish the job, open the doors, hood, trunk, tailgate, and/or fuel filler cap and wipe the inner edges of the doors and the sills dry. You're done.

Polish and Wax

After the carwash, you may want to polish and wax your vehicle. All it takes is a shady spot and an hour or so of your time.

First, let's differentiate between polish and wax. Polish is a cleaner designed to remove stubborn dirt and light oxidation (oxidation happens when the air dulls the paint). Wax is a protective coating applied to the paint to repel dirt, grime, and ultraviolet light and prevent oxidation.

So, if you car is new, or at least newer, and the paint is still in shiny, like-new condition, just use wax. Modern automotive waxes, whether liquid or paste, are much easier to apply than they were in the past. No longer do you have to rub it on, wait until it dries to a white powder, and then virtually scrub it off with a towel. Now, just wipe the wax on, wait 30–60 seconds, and buff it off. Applying the wax with an electrically powered orbital polisher not only makes the job much easier, but you'll also be the envy of your entire neighborhood. Expect to have to retrieve the polisher from a neighbor every time you want to use it.

Again, you don't have to wait until modern wax is fully dry before buffing it off. The key is a perfectly clean surface and a modern wax or sealant. Sealants tend to incorporate polymers for added protection and that wonderful wet look.

Polishing Your Car

But what if the paint on your vehicle isn't quite new anymore? That's where the term "polish" comes into play. Polishes are cleaners that can help restore that new look by removing light oxidation that tends to dull the paint. Polishes can also remove that buildup or film of road debris, dead bugs, tar, and other junk that sticks to the paint on our vehicles.

For the enthusiast, it's a 1-2-3 process. Wash, polish, wax. For those with somewhat less enthusiasm, shorten the task to a simple 1-2—wash, polish/wax. Products listed as a cleaner/wax are made for precisely this purpose, as they contain both a polish to clean the surface and a wax to protect it. They do an excellent job in both departments, so you don't have to feel guilty about skipping the polish step.

Removing Bug Goo

If you've spent this extra hour or so with your vehicle, you'll have noticed a few defects in the paint, a chip here, nick there, door ding, rust flake, even stubborn hard-to-remove bug debris, or road tar. To dissolve and remove stuff stuck on the surface of the paint, try a liquid automotive bug/tar/adhesive remover. You'll find this product near the waxes and polishes at the auto parts store.

Fixing Paint Damage

Modern automotive paint consists of a layer containing the color pigments and a clear layer on top. It's called the base coat/clear coat system, and it's much more durable than previous automotive paints. The clear coat is tougher and more scratch/damage resistant simply because it has not been diluted with any color pigments, and it's more repairable, as well.

When you find a small area of damage on the paint, inspect it carefully. If it appears to be just a line or scratch with no change in color, it's probably just in the outer clear coat. If there's a color change in the ding or scratch, both the clear and base coats have been damaged. If the primer shows through, both layers have been penetrated, and if there's any rust showing, the damage has reached the sheet metal itself.

Prioritize the importance of the repair by the depth of damage. If there's any rust or bare metal showing, fix it now.

But let's start with a very light scratch in the just the clear coat. Try the polish or cleaner/wax first, then an automotive swirl-mark remover. A very light polishing compound might help, but try it on a hidden area of paint first to make sure it doesn't dull the clear coat.

Often, the lightest of scratches will disappear with a good polishing and waxing. If they don't and you still want them to disappear, it's possible to lightly sand the clear coat with 600-grit or finer sandpaper to remove just enough material to eliminate the scratch. If you haven't already figured this out, this task is best left to an automotive professional at a detail or body shop. Like the warnings say, don't try this at home . . . unless you don't really care if your handiwork shows!

Using Touch-Up Paint

If the scratch or ding has completely penetrated the clear coat and is into the color coat, primer, or even down to bare metal, it's time for touch-up paint—or a professional repair/repaint. Step one of a DIY touch-up job is to apply masking tape to isolate the area of damage/repair and to prevent you from turning a tiny little spot of rust into a huge area of paint damage. The tape marks the boundary of your repair, so that no matter how badly you botch things, the damage won't be any bigger.

The simplest touch-up repair starts with buying either a small bottle or aerosol can of the correct color touch-up paint. Resist using the aerosol as a spray—remember the masking tape concept of limiting the size of the repair. If the paint is only available in an aerosol, just spray a small amount into a paper cup and use a very small paint or fingernail-polish brush to apply.

Try to wick the paint into the scratch or ding, rather than brushing it on with a wide stroke. You're trying to fill the "V," or valley of damage, do not cover it with a stripe of paint. This may take a couple of tries, and letting the paint thicken a bit before application can help on door scratches and other dings on vertical surfaces. If you mess up, no problem, just wipe off the paint with a clean rag dampened in that automotive bug/tar/adhesive remover, and start over.

Door Ding Repair

If the damaged area is a bit larger, perhaps a door ding from the moron in the parking lot, or if there's any bare metal or rust showing, the project will be just a bit bigger. But remember to border it off with tape first so it won't get any bigger. To remove small areas of rust, cut a 1/4-inch square of 600-grit sandpaper, stick it onto the eraser end of a pencil—spit actually works pretty well—and carefully sand away any rust or scale in the wound. If there's still brown showing after this intricate sanding, apply a small dab of rust converter—a special product that treats rust by converting it to a hard enamel-like surface. Like all things automotive, rust converter products are available at . . . your local auto parts store.

You may want to add a dab of automotive primer if there's still any bare metal showing. Again, you can spray an aerosol primer into a paper cup and apply it with a small brush. Now you're ready to apply the color.

When done properly, these DIY minor paint/body repairs are covered by the special 5/50 warranty—they won't be visible when the vehicle is traveling at 5 or more miles-per-hour or is more than 50 feet away. And that's good enough for most of us. Besides, you're doing this more to protect from rust and additional damage than to restore the vehicle's look.

Fix It Yourself or Take It to a Shop?

Is there a yardstick, or criteria, for deciding whether to repair a small area of damage or not? And whether it's a DIY project or best left to an automotive professional?

Do it yourself if the vehicle is older, already showing signs of age/mileage, and you're not obsessive about its appearance. Your only real concern is slowing/stopping any additional rust or corrosion to prolong the functional life and value of the vehicle. And if you've got the time, inclination, and willingness to try.

Leave it to the pros if . . . anything else! If the vehicle is new or newer, you want to keep it as perfect as possible, the area of damage is larger than a minor scratch, chip or ding, or you're obsessive about your vehicle's appearance. Or better yet, if someone else is going to pay for the work, such as an insurance claim or repair.

Whew! Is all this effort at keeping the outside of your vehicle clean, shiny, and rust free worth the effort? Bottom line: Only you can decide this. Remember the lesson from the car dealer: appearance is everything. In terms of residual value when it comes time to sell or trade your vehicle, if it's clean, shiny, and free of even minor body/paint damage, it's going to be worth significantly more than if it's dirty, chipped, dinged, and rusty—a lot more! ■

Project 47
Clean Upholstery and Carpet

TALENT: 1

TIME: 15–30 minutes

TOOLS: Appropriate auto-grade upholstery cleaner

COST: $6–$15

TIP: Vacuum first to remove loose dirt and avoid rubbing it into the area to be cleaned.

1 Vacuum the stain to lift off any of the substance that will come up, along with dirt and dust, which you don't want to grind in.

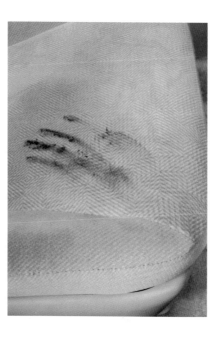

2 Spray what remains of the stain with a foam upholstery cleaner. These typically call for liberal application.

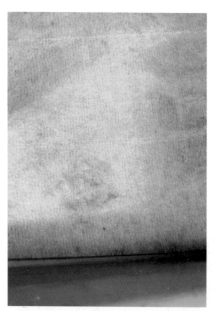

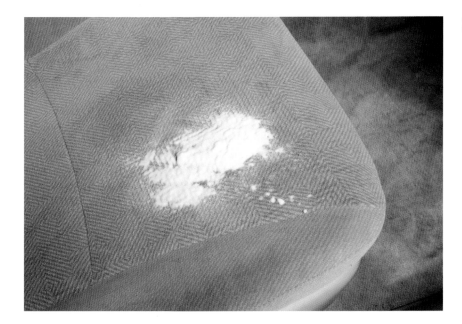

3 Let the cleaner do its work for the required period. This one said a few minutes.

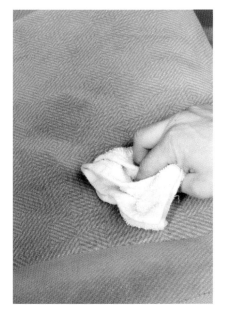
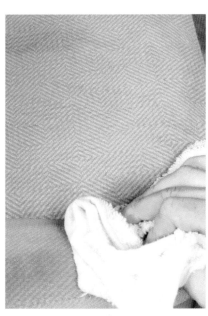

4 Then wipe with a clean, damp cloth or brush (use what the product recommends).

Vacuuming plus the foam cleaner removed virtually all of the dirty/dusty/grimy stain on this Honda's seat.

5 The same cleaner that treats automotive upholstery often works on carpets. The procedure is the same.

6 First spray on liberally and allow it to soak in.

7 Wipe off with a damp cloth or brush.

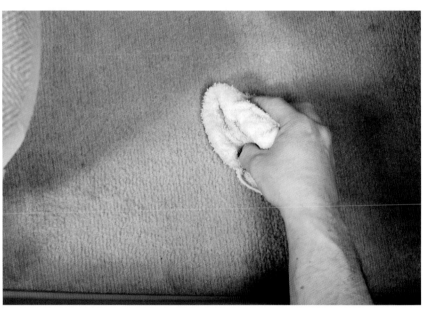

8 As with the upholstery, a good result.

Project 48
Clean Glass

TALENT: 1

TIME: 15–45 minutes, depending on number of windows and amount of dirt

TOOLS: Clean, lint-free rags, window cleaner

COST: $5–$15

TIP: Clean glass catches less light from oncoming headlights and improves night visibility.

1 A good carwash will clean the outside of your vehicle, but the interior glass also gets dirty. Some of this comes from the outside and some is the result of off-gassing by such things as the vinyl dashboard, which leaves a greasy film on windows. Fingerprints and dog nose prints add to the obstruction. Removing all this makes for a much nicer view.

2 Any good commercial glass cleaner will do. Aerosol automotive glass cleaners offer the advantage of foaming, so that they don't run down the glass. Apply it with a lint-free cloth and wipe the entire surface, including all the corners.

Be careful not to damage defroster wire grid or inside of rear window.

Project 49
Wash and Wax Car

TALENT:	2
TIME:	45–60 minutes
TOOLS:	Hose, sponge, bucket, rags, car wash soap, car wax
COST:	Materials
TIP:	Wash in the shade if you can, and use water the same temperature as the car's surface to avoid rapid expansion or contraction of the paint.

1 Washing your car is the single easiest way to keep it looking good, preserve the finish, and maintain its value.

2 Rinse off the car from top to bottom to loosen the dirt.

3 With a car wash detergent foamed up in a bucket of room/outdoor temperature water, soap the car from top to bottom with a sponge, rinsing the sponge often in the bucket.

TIP: Don't use dish or laundry soap, which are too harsh and not formulated for automotive finishes.

4 Rinse from the top down to flush the soap off the car.

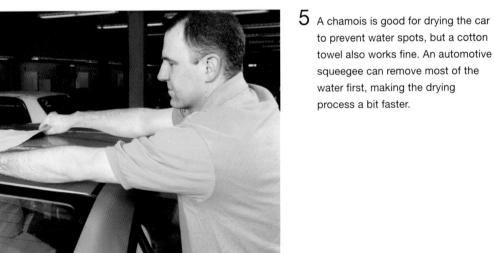

5 A chamois is good for drying the car to prevent water spots, but a cotton towel also works fine. An automotive squeegee can remove most of the water first, making the drying process a bit faster.

6 Be sure to wash and dry inside the doors, hood, hatchback or trunk, and gas filler cap.

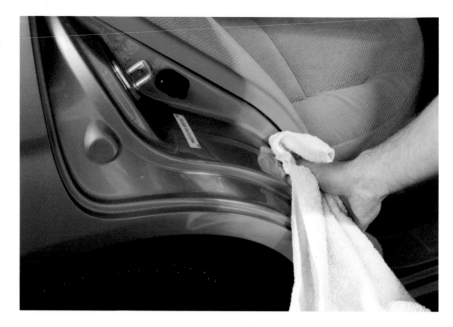

7 When the car is completely clean, apply wax and wipe it over the surface as recommended.

8 If you're not entering the car in a car show, just taking the time to wipe the wax on and buff it off is more important than any particular technique.

9 Buff the wax off with a soft cloth, turning the cloth often to a clean portion.

10 Your washed and waxed vehicle is now resistant to sun, chemicals, bird droppings, and other corrosive and damaging materials.

WASH AND WAX CAR

Project 50

Touch-Up Chips and Scratches

TALENT:	3
TIME:	1–2 hours, depending on coats
TOOLS:	Touch-up paint, fine-point brush
COST:	$10–$20
TIP:	Several light, even applications work better than one heavy coat.

1 Little scratches and chips not only detract from a car's looks, they also expose the metal underneath to rust. Touch-up paint can help to protect against corrosion.

2 Wash the area and dry it fully. Then wipe it with something to remove oils and grease, like rubbing alcohol or an automotive bug/tar/adhesive remover, which is available at the auto parts store.

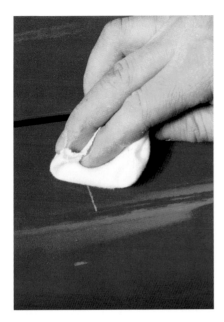

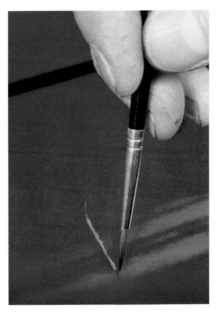

3 The little brush that comes with the touch-up paint is inaccurate and odds are you won't be satisfied with the results. Go to a hobby or hardware store and buy a brush with a nice fine point. If the only touch-up paint you can find comes in an aerosol form, spray a small amount of paint into a paper cup, then use your brush to apply.

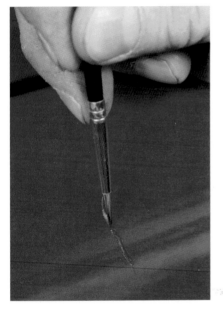

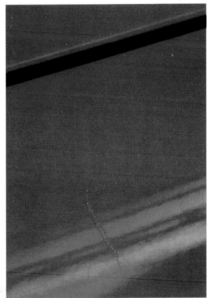

4 Dip just the tip of the brush into the paint and, with a steady hand, make a single stroke to fill the scratch. Do it all in one motion and try to keep the paint within the scratch. The paint will flow and spread out to fill it.

5 Allow the paint to dry for the recommended period. This paint calls for 30 minutes between coats. Clean your brush with paint thinner and wipe it dry it between coats.

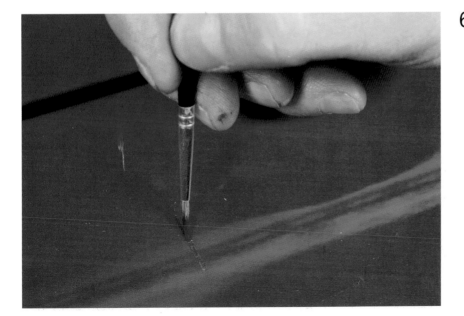

6 Apply another coat. Use just a little paint and apply it in one motion.

TOUCH-UP CHIPS AND SCRATCHES

7 Allow to dry, again cleaning and drying your brush while you wait.

8 This was three light passes over the scratch. It isn't flawless, but it looks much better than prior to the repair and is all but invisible more than a few feet from the car.

TIP: If the chip or scratch you're trying to repair has any rust in it, use a small piece of sandpaper to remove the rust. Try sticking it to the eraser of a new pencil for accurate sanding. Then use a thin layer of rust converter or primer, followed by paint.

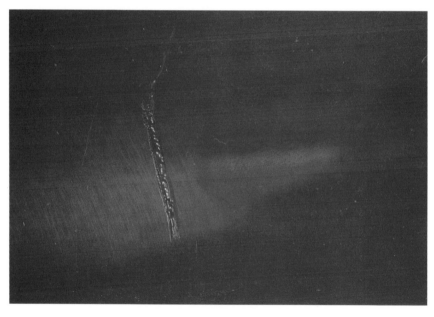